1921: Swiss racers Colle and Parel take a break in Dalstein, Moselle, where the Tour draws its spectators to their doorways.

Graphic design and production: Jean Marie Hatier
All photos:

PRESSE **E** SPORTS
Agence d'images   *groupe l'Équipe*

Original French Edition, Le Tour de France Intime by Philippe Brunel
Published by © CALMANN-LEVY, 1995. 3 Rue Auber, 75009 Paris, France.
Translation from French provided by: Lois Lovett
Worldwide English rights held by Buonpane Publications,
a division of Colorado Creative Media, Inc.
P.O. Box 40724, Denver, CO 80204-0724 U.S.A.
(01) (303) 831-0917
ISBN 0-9649835-0-8

AN INTIMATE PORTRAIT OF THE TOUR DE FRANCE

Philippe Brunel

In the old days, Hugo Koblet chased after women as avidly as he went after the day's yellow jersey, Gino Bartali smoked cigarettes under his coach Coppi's nose and Jacques Anquetil rarely went anywhere without Janine, his platinum blonde "Dame Blanche". Champions mixed their private life with that of the Tour de France without fear of exposure, and the close quarters injected a heady dose of romanticism into the story of the race. There were no cameras, no cordless microphones, no drug tests. The racers performed under the conniving and affectionate eye of the sportswriters, such as Antoine Blondin, who was always drunk "with the joy of bicycle racing," they said euphemistically, and always prolific, "he drank ink and peed copy," as the argot had it. Those were the blessed days when cycling inspired purple prose from Trenet, Emile Prudhomme and Aime Barelli.

We each carry our own Tour de France inside us. Ours is full of thundering names, like the names of warriors, saints, and bullfighters: Guido Reybroeck, Martin Van den Bossche, Federico Bahamontes, Tomaso De Pra, Julio Jiminez, Herman Van Springel, Italo Zilioli. For ages, our Tour meant the France of paid vacations, village centers full of crowds, Postillon wine and

Nivea cream. As the pack passed by, fire hoses sprayed rain across the fiery skies of July. We also had Pellos' drawings of Jacques Goddet in colonial garb, the railway cafe at Coutances, Luis Ocana at the Laffrey coast, his chin in stitches after a fall in the Alsatian hills, Luis Ocana again, crucified by a storm in the Mente pass. We had Merckx doffing his cap at the monument marking where the great Simpson fell, Perrier at the finish line, flasks of Evian water, the voices of Fernand Choisel, Guy Kedia and Jean Paul Brouchon crooning "A vous la route du Tour" (the Tour's route is yours). And then there was Chapatte commentating on television year-after-year, the initials HD on the wool jerseys sponsored by Virlux, and Anquetil and Merckx, were always there, they had to be, and they're still there, for the Tour is a sentimental thing. Anquetil didn't leave the Tour in 1966 near Saint Etienne. In our minds, he's still out in front, surely in the first four; he's going to beat Indurain and get back the yellow jersey -- his jersey, and Merckx's too. If style makes a man, it makes a champion too, and in this area Anquetil and Merckx will never be rivaled.

We thought we knew everything about the Tour and its apostles: the racers, organizers, sporting directors and reporters. We

never saw these champions as they appear here: candidly stripped down in broad daylight, their bodies being loosened by a masseur's hands, avowed enemies sharing a bath, letting themselves go at last. We see them living in the poignant glow of the stages' evenings, as if through a two-way mirror. They show themselves rid of their star status, as simple family men, just regular guys. They are ordinary, sublime and at times pathetic all at once.

These photographs, snatched from oblivion, show an intimate and unknown Tour de France, the lost moments of the Tour. From Ottavio Bottecchia to Miguel Indurain, a portrait emerges here of the men who forced open the door of our imagination through their talent or their vulnerability.

Today the Tour, so tightly constrained by its own popularity, has lost some of its charm. It has become one of the year's big media events, and the racers have become temporary actors, expected to come up with subtle repartee worthy of the satirist Sacha Guitry. Hounded by the press, eager to be alone, the big stars hide themselves away in their hotel rooms once evening comes, skirting the cities where the Tour has become cut off from its fame and the frank humanity it once effused as it went by.

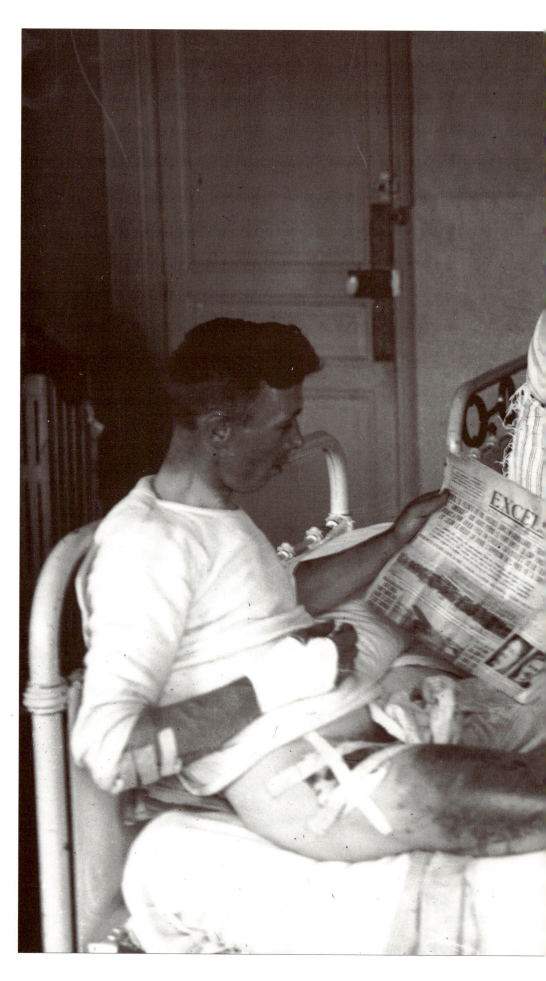

We could swear they were burn victims, but they were only racers at the end of a very hot and highly contested day.

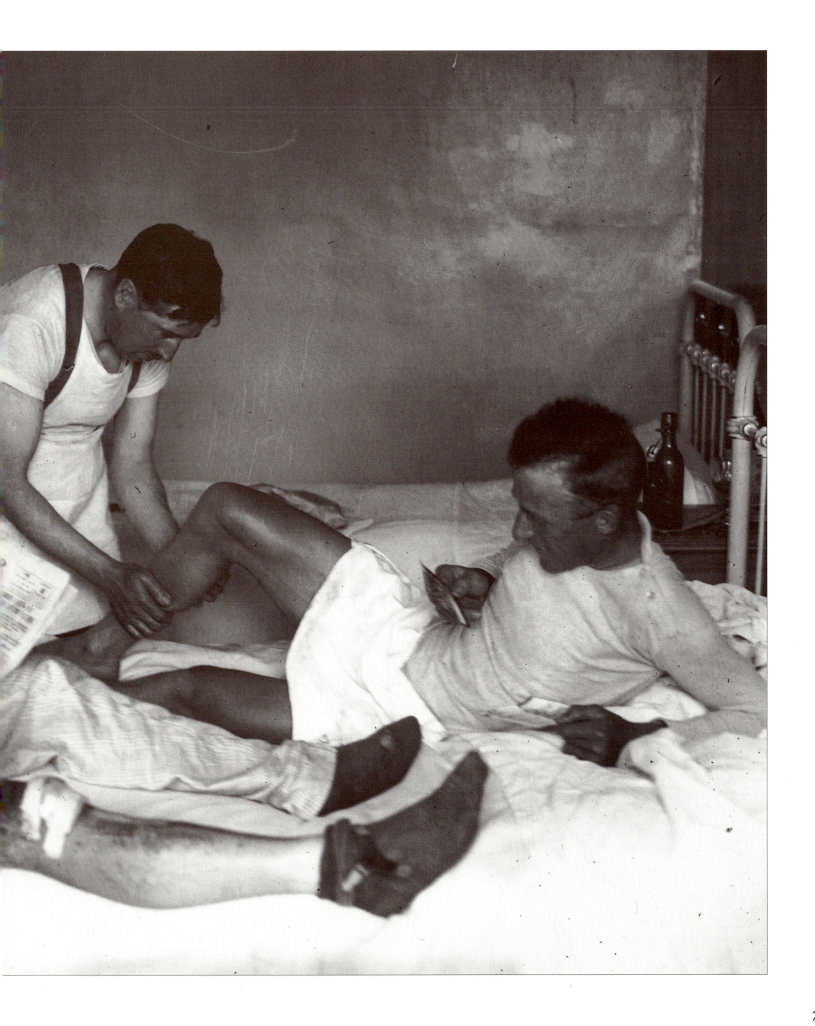

The chase to the canteen, where the expression "fugitive of the Tour de France" was born.

The Tours heroes and their recreation: Deloffre was the acrobat, Vervaeke and Geldhol smoked the cigarette.

Ottavio Bottecchia in full effort.
His star did not shine long but it
had an intense luminosity.

OTTAVIO BOTTECCHIA

When the farmer discovered him and came to his aid in the hot noonday sun, as the countryside began to retreat from the heat, Lorenzo di Santolo realized that he recognized this man from Belfort, this man who was in agony in his arms. He laid the man out on his back and removed the dust from his face. It was Ottavio Bottecchia. His bicycle was leaning against a post without a scratch on it, nor showing any traces of damage from a fall. But Bottecchia's inert body was covered with scratches, and broken from one side to the other. His helmut was red with blood.

The death of a champion never passes without evoking strong emotions, but the death of Ottavio Bottecchia was accompanied by a mystery that remains unsolved to this day. Sixty-eight years later we find ourselves still searching for answers. Was he stoned by grape growers furious because he had pilfered a few grapes? Was he run over by a car and accidently killed or was he the victim of a Fascist plot -- he was not one who hid his Socialistic views.

Investigators concluded that it was an accidental death. From their viewpoint he had become uncomfortable after gulping down a cold drink and as he tried to remove himself from his "cale pieds" (foot stirrups), he fell, striking his head on a sharp rock, which knocked him out. Regaining consciousness, he pursued his way to help weaving along the road until he reached the village of Peonis where he collapsed on the grass in front of Lorenzo di Santelo's home.

This story was confirmed by three credible witnesses; by the farmer di Santelo, by his wife, Domenica, who transported him in a small cart to Gemone Hospital, swearing she heard him whisper the words "malore, malore" (it hurts, it hurts). The third witness was his niece Elena, to whom he apparently told the details of the "accident" during a brief period of consciousness.

However, twenty years later in the New York City borough of Manhattan, a man who had been stabbed on the docks and was lying there in agony, confessed his heinous crime -- that it was he who had killed the famed Italian champion "under

The sands of time have not erased the exploits of the Italian, found dead on a country road in 1927.

contract" before he came to the United States. He even provided the name of the man who ordered the hit, which was Berto Olinas. No trace of this person was ever found. A further troubling fact arose: in 1973, the pastor of Peonis *Don* (Father) Dante Nigris, as he lay in his own death-bed, confessed to *Don* Nello Marcuzzi, that Bottecchia had been beaten to death by a group of Fascists, who were infuriated by his success in sports. Later Marcuzzi would write, "Everything we can say to date is without proof. The champion's death was the result of a political plot." In 1985 the champion's daughter Maria Fortunata

declared in the newspaper *Il Piccolo de Trieste* "never exclude the possibility of murder", especially after the reporter Giulo Crosti revealed the results of his own investigation. Here is what he discovered: 'In the hours following di Santolo's discovery of the inert body of the champion, the Gemone Police Sergeant was summoned to the office of the local Fascist Militia Chief and given the order to make the report of Bottecchia's death appear to be a common accident'.

"Whom to believe and what kind of grapes can be eaten in June?" were questions posed by Armando Cougnet, which

reinforced the mystery of the death. Two reporters, Giardini and Garatti reconstructed the fateful day of June 3, 1927 as follows: The champion arose at dawn and asked his niece Elena a favor, which was to go and ask her mother to 'prepare a hot bath for me, one that will last for three hours'.

Bottecchia was in an excellent mood. His only regret that day was that his companion and friend Alfonso Piccin could not come with him as he trained. Later on the family learned that after his supposed "fall" in Peonis he was carried by some men to a church ostiary, who summoned the priest, *Don* Dante Nigris, and this priest

gave him the last rites. From there he was brought to Gemone Hospital, where Dr. Rieppi diagnosed a fracture at the base of the skull, another fracture of the clavicle and many black and blue marks. Professor Giordino from Venice was also present during the examination and he wrote his testimony in the hospital log book, but he neglected mention of the beating theory.

It was out of the question to think of Bottecchia as an anti-Fascist. Even if he did not agree with the Mussolini theory, the Friulian champion had become an excellent role model for the "New Italy". He became it's "poster boy" defining the Italian propaganda machine's exultation of the grandiose reconstructive and cultural efforts of Italy at that time.

In 1923 the Italian newspaper *Gazetta* had launched a national subscription drive which netted a profit of 61,275 lira. Spearheading the drive as the first new subscriber was the champion himself. For that reason, Bottecchia was considered a first class Fascist by some. Remember at that time and in that imbroglio it was difficult to define or separate right from wrong. Four years after the official subscription effort, for whatever reason, the regime was too preoccupied with more pressing problems than to try and suppress a champion of such stature, who seemed so politically unconnected. This fact was underlined by an important political observer of that time.

Another side of Bottecchia that no one could ignore was his health problems. He suffered constant back pain. He coughed as though his lungs would tear themselves apart. His career was stagnating and not up to the level of his young rival by the name of Binda. He feared becoming too attached to his opponent and realized that it would not help him beat his competitor, if he became too close a friend.

Ottavio confided to his friend and neighbor at Pordenone, Alfonso Piccin, that he wished to see a physician the same day that the drama unfolded. Later, no one would believe the official theory about "discomfort" after gulping a cold drink. According to most observers the family accepted the convenient version, fearing adverse consequences should they balk, and to be sure they needed the 500,000 lira life insurance policy which they could not receive if the accident was a result of a professional accident or as a result of cycling training.

Ottavio was born to a family of nine children that had had to emigrate to Belgium so they could find work in the mines of Charleroi. They returned to Italy "poor maybe, but at least in our own country". Had it not been for the war of 1914 to 1918, Bottecchia would not have had to leave his native village of San Martino di Colle Umberto. Prior to the war he worked as a brick layer and was happy to be with his family. He was very proud of his hands -- so strong and calloused -- and enjoyed showing them off to his friends and colleagues. He married a country girl by the name of Caterina Zambon

and she gave him three children, Giovanna, Maria Fortuneta, and Danilo.

He was drafted into the elite corps of sharpshooters who transported themselves on bicycles. He was captured three times by Austrian troops. On the third time he escaped he brought back with him a machine gun for the Italian troops. Upon his safe return he was given a bronze medal for his courage under fire and for inflicting severe damage on the Austrian troops which halted their advance. Bottecchia welcomed the medal without being effusive about it, because he was not one to be materialistic about such things. What he needed to do was support his family. He took on odd jobs. He became a teamster and then began a transporting business before the economic crisis of the times forced him to sell his horses.

This was the turning point of his life and it was accentuated by the explosion of Fascism.

At the legislative elections, Mussolini received 65% of the vote. The leader seemed to fanaticize his crowds. His power became so strong that he had his rival, Deputy Matteoti, assassinated.

In his quest for independence, Bottecchia turned to another life pursuit discovered by the poor: bicycle racing. His first trial results encouraged him to head in that direction. Indeed, he won his first race by such a large margin that his fellow racers suspected he had taken a short cut.

Bottecchia surmised "evidently one does not need an aptitude for this job", so he embraced it with the belief of youth, his warrior belief, which had stood him well during the war. In 1923 he finished fifth in the Tour d'Italie race which was won by Girardengo, the first champion in Italian history and the six-time winner of Milan-San Remo. A reporter named Borrela noticed Bottecchia and encouraged him to accept

On the road, the shadow of a doubt was born on the coattails of the racers.

Bottecchia's supporters did not hesitate to cross the Alps to encourage him in his efforts. He was the first Italian winner of the Tour in 1924 and 1925.

the invitation of the French group Automoto, who for commercial reasons wanted to have one or two Italians in their group. Bottecchia followed Borrelo's advice and granted his services to Henri and Francis Pelissier, who graciously welcomed him.

In France the comments voiced irony. "Why take this Bottecchia?" and "There's a strange choice!" Most of the critics were skeptical of this enigmatic racer with the sad, Don Quixote kind of face summarized as "straight body and thin face". They

ignored the fact that the Italian was a first-class climber. That year, the Friulian (the man from Friulia) won the second stage of the Havre-Cherbourg race, autographed the yellow jersey and gave it back to Henri Pelissier. The Galiber ascension permitted

him to consolidate his second place in the general classification statistics. In Paris, Henri Pelissier predicted that Bottecchia would have a brilliant career. He stated "Bottecchia has the look of a country boy, but in cycling ... what style! He has arms and legs that never stop. I doubt anyone has taught him anything useful, but for sure he looks good on a bicycle. All of him is made for cycling, plus he has class". We'll return to that later.

In his last editorial, Henri Desgrange praised him by saying "We cannot conclude this Tour without coming back to Italy's taciturn Bottecchia. We know that he gave back the yellow jersey to Pelissier but he was in the hunt everyday and never gave a poor showing and that performance shows that it could only be realized by a man with class. On the Col de l'Izoard it was said that he missed practice (he could not always resist his thirst) but he always showed his ability on the bottom line. He was couragious and tenacious in the mountains. Bottecchia is the most sensational revelation of that Tour. Without knowing our language, he has shown the qualities of a real champion. You can imagine him next year, when he will be better prepared. Stronger from his first experience, and you will see that he will generously show more of his talent."

Henri Desgrange's prediction proved true the following year. Bottecchia won the Tour and wore the yellow jersey from beginning to end, except for the portion of the race at Briancon where he was wearing

a purple jersey, which he preferred because it was one of his own brand. The evening before the race, in Toulon, the Italian received a warning letter at his hotel. "You are an anti-Fascist, you will be punished" his mysterious writer had written. Many times he had found his tires flat at the very beginning of a race. Many a time he had signed an autograph and when he turned back around his tires would be flat. During the race he would suffer from dust in the eyes, all the while dominating his competitors. His most prominent one being Nicolas Frantz, who achieved a 35 minute lead over the Friulian. On the mountain he broke the record for that time period. No one could catch him or pass him. "It would be dangerous to follow him up a mountain pass, it would be suicidal", said Frantz. "His progression is so powerful and regular that we would end up asphyxiated."

The day after his big victory, an enthusiastic crowd arrived to greet him at the Milan Central train station. All eyes were fixed on the first class cars, but Bottecchia appeared from a third class compartment, dressed simply, wearing a grey suit with a light patched cotton shirt and carrying a cardboard suitcase. In the troubled game of fame and glory he knew exactly how to keep his feet on the ground. In San Martino di Colle Umberto, he never started his training regimen before taking care of his family duties as a husband and father first. To stay with his family longer he turned down offers from Italian organizers, who proposed to him a salary far inferior to what he received in France and ridiculous in comparison to what Girardengo and Brunero earned.

In 1925 he won the Tour de France again acquiring double notoriety, but then the troubles began. In 1926 he gave up the Tour under a thunderstorm on the way to Bayonne-Luchon, where exactly 12 months earlier he had fired everyone's imagination. By age 32 the "old" bricklayer had received everything he wanted from cycling. Rich and popular, he gave the impression that he had lost a part of his motivation. He simply pretended to be preoccupied with thoughts of his health. "I'm afraid I'll catch a serious illness," he said to himself. He was full of dark thoughts and bad premonitions, which circled about him like a vague perfume of tragedy. In fact Henri Pelissier (the man who made famous the Albert Londres "Slaves of the Road" picture in 1924), felt Bottecchia would be felled by a shotgun blast from his wife Camille, who was enraged by the over-zealous attentions of an obsessed fan. His best friend Alfonso Piccin, crashed his motorcycle against the wall of the San Giacomo di Veglio asylum and no one knew why or what caused the accident. Finally, three months before the "fall" at Peonis, Bottecchia suffered the pain of losing his younger brother in an automobile accident.

The day of Ottavio Bottecchia's funeral, the family received numerous sympathy cards, one even from a family in Savoy, but none from the Fascist hierarchy.

The entire country wept over the death of the glorious sharpshooter, the immigrant, the first ambassador of Italian cycling, the prototypical racer, he who symbolized the expression of their national revival. He had not been compromised nor corrupted by fame or fortune. They would celebrate his nobility and his patriotism. They spoke of him as though he was a magnificent thoroughbred. They saluted the adventure of the athlete, who confronts his job and the roads of the Tour de France with the same courage which had made him a hero in the war. They expressed pain and regret for not celebrating him as he deserved. Before he collapsed on that country road on June 3, 1927, Bottecchia had confided his desire to finish his career by racing his last season in Italy, and for that reason his death seemed so unfair. He died before receiving the proper respect of his countrymen. He died after conquering poverty and acquiring comfort and contentment with himself. "Bad luck took it's revenge. Italy is today deprived of one of it's sons, a man who honored his country even outside it's borders," wrote Guissepe Ambrosini in Paese. "The sport itself has lost a famous champion. Bottecchia is no longer here with us but his memory will be with us forever."

The Friulian was back on Contadini soil, his homeland, that soil that had seen him born and raised.

In the game of racing, there was both trouble and glory, but he kept his feet on the ground.

It would not be proper to call him a handsome man. Bottecchia wore a mask of tragedy. He was like a Don Quixote, unbending in his principles, but he was one of the most beautiful climbers of the Tour.

In 1924, in a restaurant of Coutances, Albert Londres assists in the abandon of the brothers Pelissier, in a revolt against the Tour organizers. "We are treated like beasts in the circus," they declared in an address to Henri Desgrange. On his return to Cayenne, the celebrated reporter headed his article "The Slaves of the Road". The formula was to be dated. It is also the first grand media coup in the History of the Tour.

Adelin Benoit, proudly posing beside his bicycle. He embodies a "slave" at the height of his condition.

The Belgian Brackeveld in his version of a frugal lunch in the country in 1922.

The Tour in the sunshine: Gordini takes snow from a ledge, Bottecchia plunges into the running waters of a fountain.

Robert Jacquinot feeds himself in a restaurant in Hostens. The Parisien was one of the grand animators of the Tour at the beginning of the '20s.

GINO BARTALI

Tears flowed down the cheeks of his fans, who kissed the ground he walked on. Women threw rose petals and children sang carols. When he won the Liege portion of the Tour de France in 1948, Pope Pius XII heaped great praise upon him, and Milan's Archbishop came to visit him in the hospital when he fell victim to an accident on the way to Lugano's Grand Prix Race. Later on he was given a private audience with Pope Jean XXIII and Pope Paul VI, who welcomed him as a hero and an "icon" for all Italians searching for morality. With Gino Bartali there was something religious in the air, some mystical thing which brought pleasure to an Italy still suffering from its carnal years, the end of the Mussolini era with its black shirts and the eventual Italian renovation. A practicing and devout Catholic, Bartali incarnated a sort of miracle. He embodied the idea that we can elevate social and economic achievement without compromise, and distance oneself far from all temptations while generating a sense of direction. For nearly twenty years he offered up his conscience and won the respect of his countrymen. He inspired only the best thoughts among the top journalists of the time: Dino Buzzati, editor of the *Corriere della Sera,* Italio Cavino, a reporter for *Umanita* and also Curzio Malaparte, who one day wrote this statement: "In Coppi's veins gas flows, but in Bartali only blood flows." For the regime in place at that time, who cared that he was a militant Catholic or that he refused to endorse fascist ideology, Bartali was the providential flag-bearer, demonstrating how strong a winner Italy was. He needed only to wear the national team jersey and it gave the impression of the power in place. That was just what he did in the 1938 Tour de France. The champion had received a telegram from the Federation Leader, who was counting on Bartali's presence in the Grand Boucle (the Great Circle). "If Bartali is not racing in the Tour (he had just won the Giro d'Italy), what other racer could seriously represent us?" More than a question, this was an order, Bartali was convinced. He went out and won the Tour and his popularity increased. The "big name racers" of that time respected him and the man in the street identified with him. He collected fans who were rich and poor, oppressors and oppressed, and provided for that agitated period of time a moment of stability for

a country humiliated by a frustrating war. "Do not touch, he is a god", cried Sports Minister General Antonelli, as he tried to disperse the crowd when the champion won the 1938 Tour de France. They put him on a pedestal. Then one day Fausto Coppi arrived on the scene and scrambled Bartali's orderly life.

Their meeting took place on June 4, 1939 during the Piemont Tour when Bartali caught sight of an unknown, emaciated face with an exhorbitant look upon it. He befriended this newcomer and welcomed him. Under the advice of recruiter Girardengo, Parvesi recruited Coppi for Legano. The two men, the old and the new shared common ground. They were both country boys from Contadini. One from Tuscany and the other from Piemont; but both men spoke the same language and they hailed from the same region.

In 1940 Fausto Coppi was only a support racer from Florentin, when the duo went side by side in the Tour of Italy. Victory was due for Bartali but he crashed after being knocked down by a dog on the second turn. He hurt his knee badly and suffered like a martyr to the point where he could not even endure his massages. The old Tuscan continued the race and saved Coppi in the big Dolomite part of the race. Coppi won the Giro's portion, unleashing passions ordinarily reserved for the team leader. It was on this occasion that Bartali realized that he and Coppi would be competitors as well as teammates from this point on. Their rivalry wasn't really effective until after the war. During a stage of the Milan-San Remo race of 1946, Coppi achieved one of his greatest exploits: a solitary escape of 147 kilometers, which enabled him to hold off France's Tessiere by more than 15 minutes. Ten minutes after that the public along the Via Roma saw Ricci and Bartali fight an uninspiring race for third place.

"Who won?" Bartali asked. The answer left him speechless. The world of cycling had witnessed the birth of a champion. This also led to a cataclysm which could bring it all down for Bartali if he wasn't careful.

Later on, each time he beat Coppi, it gave him pleasure to light up a cigarette as soon as he crossed the finish line, adding more puffing pride to the moment as it were. Bartali usually smoked three cigarettes a day on the advice of his physician, who diagnosed it as necessary to accelerate his slow heartbeat. "I would smoke one in the morning, one after a race, and the third one in the evening before going to bed", Bartali said. "Binda kept the pack on him so on victory day, I had the right to smoke a fourth one!"

Coppi-Bartali. Bartali-Coppi. In Italy following the Mussolini era, it was impossible to side with either Coppi or Bartali. The country correctly surmised that those two celebrities, who were so different, were in essence performing the same job. For more than ten years they took on the world of cycling to a point that had everyone believing that they were the only ones occupying the stage. On one side there was Coppi, the free-thinking apostle of modernism, whose bones, when broken were like shards of glass; versus Bartali, "the Pious", the down-to-earth human being from puritan Italy, who was so committed to his Catholic faith. He was the monastic champion with the disgraceful looking legs with no apparent calves. Culzio Malaparte said of him, "Bartali belongs to those who accept the dogma. He is metaphysical. He is protected by the saints. Coppi has no one up there to take care of him." So on one side there was the aetheist (Coppi) and on the other an amusing churchgoer, who distrusted women. So much so that in the beginning of the 1938

The old Tuscan took his strength from the profound mystery of his faith. He was very committed to the Catholic faith. Here he prays next to Magni, under the watchful eyes of Gastone Nencini.

pay dearly for trying to stay up with him. In all, Bartali could lay claim to forty-three uphill Grand Prix events as opposed to the seventeen that Coppi won, and while on this subject, let's not forget that he left nearly a half hour late in the grand race of the Swiss Tour in 1947, which included the St. Bernard and the St. Gothard. Bartali and Coppi rarely showed their antagonism for one another in public. They dreaded each other and preferred to maintain a neutral stance rather than fight.

The two philosophers confounded each other. Coppi belonged to a well organized program based on a new type of diet and interval training. Within Coppi's entourage was a blind trainer named Cavanna, who followed him as he traveled, rallying for a reduction in the kilometers in the races because he felt the races were too long and tedious. Bartali, on the contrary, took advantage of the long race marathons.

It was no secret. Everyone knew that Coppi took vitamins. Behind the scenes it was felt in some circles that he was also on drugs. On the other side of the coin, Bartali was content to eat the traditional minestrone and pasta. He also indulged himself from time to time with a tall glass of grappa (wine). He remained the proudest partisan of the bicying adventure.

"Coppi's style of cycling is a style for young men", said Bartali. Intrigued by his

Tour he had refused to kiss Josephine Baker, because he was already engaged to be married. "Myself, I was shy in private but sassy in public," Bartali noted. Coppi was the opposite. We never knew what he was thinking, but inside he was in a rage. A tremendous mountain climber, he was in the same vein as Vietto, Trueba, Robec or Lazarides. On the straightaways he propelled himself with an incomparable speed that the other racers usually reserved for the downhill. One hundred meters seated, followed by one hundred meters standing up on the pedals, making the other racers

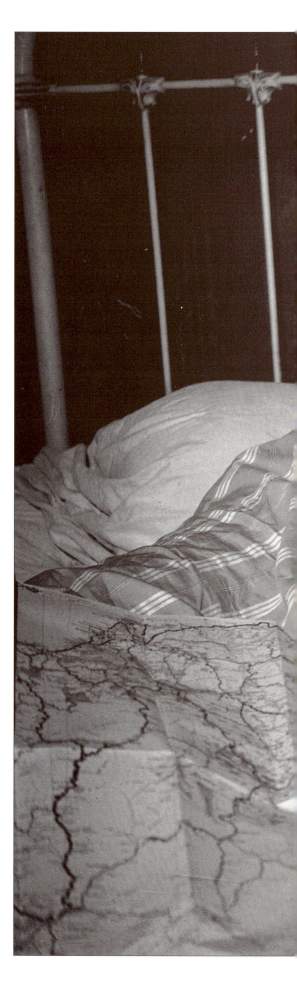

Bartali: a maniacal champion empowered by a spiritual force.

rival's new methods, he took to spying on him in detail even to the point of looking in Coppi's bedroom for anything suspicious that might provide a clue to the strange habits of the Piemontian.

"I would wait until he had left the hotel ahead of me before I inspected his bedroom," Bartali revealed some years later. "I searched the wastebasket and picked up as much as I could of everything that looked suspicious: vials, all kinds of bottles, tubes, boxes, absolutely everything." Bartali forced his teammate, Primo Volpi, to test suppositories that Coppi had had manufactured at a Genoa pharmaceutical laboratory. Another time, while returning from a Giro's Tour, he took a detour of 150 kilometers out of his way just to explore the low sides of the road on the Braco downhill, where he had seen Coppi get rid of a bottle. Suspicious of what kind of potion was in the bottle he had kept his eye on the spot where he thought the bottle had been tossed. After patient searching, he finally found the bottle and had the contents analyzed. To his amazement, he found the mysterious liquid was just a simple solution of bicarbonate of soda.

Italians respected Coppi and worshipped Bartali. The Tuscan Lion won the Piemont Tour in 1951. Coppi's younger brother Serse was irritated by Bartali's popularity. In 1952 at Giro, Bartali forced his teammate, Donato Piazza, to wear his Italian Champion's jersey and to race ahead of the group for as long as possible. Thus Piazza had all the spectators' attention focused on him while the real Italian champion remained back in the shadows.

The legend of the pious Gino was born from his victory at Lourdes in 1948. His religous devotion was not an act but rooted in fact. Each evening he placed a small statue of the Virgin Mary on his night stand. Upon the death of his brother Giulio, who was killed during the race in 1936 (and possibly the reason why he initially felt so close to Coppi), he went two months without touching his bicycle and thought seriously about retiring from cycling entirely. During the war, he was the messenger for the Catholic Party, for which he never stopped fighting. It was Bartali again, who carried the Olympic torch to the Ghisallo church. At Lourdes, his victory appeared almost too symbolic because his winning the race was not at all expected. Gino came out of the race with no problems but lost in the Tour of Italy, which was won by Fiorenzo Magni. At age 34 it was said that Bartali was finished, that his career was on the skids. Winner of the Paris-Trouville first stage of the race, he took 24th place in the general classifications, 21 minutes ahead of Louison Bobet. In the morning of the seventh stage of the Biarritz-Lourdes race, he came back, confounding almost everyone who had prematurely buried him. That day, the day of his comeback, Bobet and Robic could do nothing against him. The Italian appeared to be ordained with grace from above, carried along by an extra spirit and protected by the Madonna herself. At the departure from Lourdes Monsignor Theas praised Bartali and this praise was later imposed on the Toulouse sidewalk in front of Guy LaPebie and Stan Ockers. He showed

more cycling prowess in the Alps, winning three new races: at Braincon, Aix-les-Bains, and Liege. At Cannes, the phone woke him up while he was in bed. "Mr. Bartali, it's for you," the concierge shouted. "For me?" Gino said. He did not like to be disturbed in the evening. Even his wife herself did not dare to disturb him after supper, but he thought this must be her. Adriana had called him earlier from Florence to inform him of the political situation there. She had been extremely preoccupied during the conversation, due to the fact that Communist Party Secretary Palmiro Togliatti had been wounded by extremist gunfire. The country was teetering on the edge of insurrection. So Bartali was quite surprised to hear the voice of his friend, Deputy Alcide de Gaspari, the future leader of the Christian Democratic Party, say to him, "Gino ... we need you".

His caller did not act like he usually did when they conversed. He seemed ner-

vous. "But what can I do? I'm here to race in the next stage of the Tour de France," said Bartali. "Exactly," said de Gaspari, "you can do a lot by winning that stage," he stated, trying to convince Bartali to try and outdo himself. "If you win it, it will create a diversion. It will motivate people towards happy feelings. A distraction. Believe me...we all need it". The ploy worked.

After pondering it for a moment, the old Gino came back with, "Listen ... I will do even better than that. I will win the entire Tour de France race."

Bartali fought hail in the Croix de Fer and floods in the Chartreuse portion of the Tour, but he won. The effect on the public by his victory revealed the most superior political strategy of the time. At Briancon, he provoked the admiration of his fans, especially Jacques Goddet, who wrote in his Tour Director's notes: "From snowstorm, water, ice, Bartali arose majes-

tically like an angel covered with mud, wearing under his soaked tunic the precious soul of an exceptional champion. It took this day of apocalypse to express the total quality of this Italian champion. Let's greet this racer!" He added, "overwhelmed by their hearty efforts one-by-one each man ran out of energy and collapsed under Bartali's relentless pressure. He became once again the dazzling magician of the summits, flying on the mountains, reducing to nothing all those who, moments before, were his adversaries. On this execrable planet his gracious pedaling couldn't help but exhort admiration."

Between his first victory in the Grand Boucle (Big Circle) in 1938, and his second in 1948, ten years had passed. Italy had survived profound upsets; the downfall of Mussolini, the defeat of Fascism in 1945, and the return to democracy marked by agricultural reform. At the movie theatre one can see the apparition of the neo-real-

He enchanted the Tour and won it twice at ten-year intervals.

With Henri Desgrange, the father of the Tour.

ism. One world chasing another, and in this mutation Gino Bartali remains true to himself. He continued to symbolize genuine patriotism and devotion to the Catholic Church, and presented a fundamental, stable view of the culture now in progress. Bartali like any other man was capable of tricks. Thus he was involved from the very beginning in the mass desertion of the Transalpins in the 1950 Tour de France.

It was a terrible blow to the morale of the Italian team, who were responsible for demonstrating a certain hostility towards the French in the Val d'Aoste in 1949. The press suspected Fiorenzo Magni's soldiers and the Bartali squadron of joining forces in a common cause, namely hostility towards the French. An incident took place at the top of Aspin, where an overexcited fan, trying to hold Bartali's hand actually caused him and also Robic to fall. The Italian exchanged insults, some more or less hurtful, others irreparable and the organizers had to intervene so Bartali could start again. Minutes after crossing the finish line, in the pouring rain, he announced his withdrawal from the race.

"We were attacked, consequently we will not be going out tomorrow," Bartali declared to the reporters. Organizers tried to reason with him. They set up headquarters at his hotel in Loures-Barousse. Jacques Goddet talked about diverting the race towards Menton and also promised to furnish Bartali with security in the form of 20 armed policemen. As a last resort, Goddet suggested to Bartali that he wear a grey jersey, so he could pass unnoticed. Immediately Bartali became furious. "If I have the courage to start again, it will be in the tricolor and not anything else!", he fumed. "I am Italian and intend to stay Italian!"

He turned towards Alfredo Binda and the two men, who trained the squadron and the cadets after their retirements went their way without regret, because Fiorenzo Magni had seized the yellow jersey. To the *Gazetta* reporter, the Tuscan confided his irritation. He could not stand how the French press treated him, and all Italian racers for that matter, with names like "wheel suckers". "Everyday we take risks. People throw dirt and stones at us, they try to put branches between our spokes, going further would be like heading into a

slaughterhouse". Gino simply seized on this incident as a pretext to leave a race which was already in his disfavor after Fiorenzo Magni seized power. Already beaten by Coppi in 1949, he was afraid to become destitute at the hands of the young cadet. He preferred to give up rather than engage in combat on the racing field. On the Tour there were many Bartali-types, all rivals of Coppi for sure. There was the Florentine, Gino Machievel, who in 1950 ridiculed the cycling world by beating Van Steenbergen in the final stage of the Milan-San Remo by deceiving the Belgian at the finish line.

Bartali was then 36 years old. It was he, who had signed with Coppi in 1949 a non-aggression pact, pretending to sacrifice his pride for the honor of their country, even though he admitted the superiority of his young rival. Finally it was Bartali, as always, who moved racing fans everywhere, by spontaneously offering his wheel in the 1952 Tour, to the Piemontian, in front of the TV cameras, making sure his gesture did not go unnoticed.

Gino the Pious never did anything completely for free...

Fausto Coppi, in the plaid shirt, at the table of his squadron. The Piemontais had discovered the benefits of a strict diet at a time when the majority of the Transalpins ate a hearty minestrone.

FAUSTO COPPI

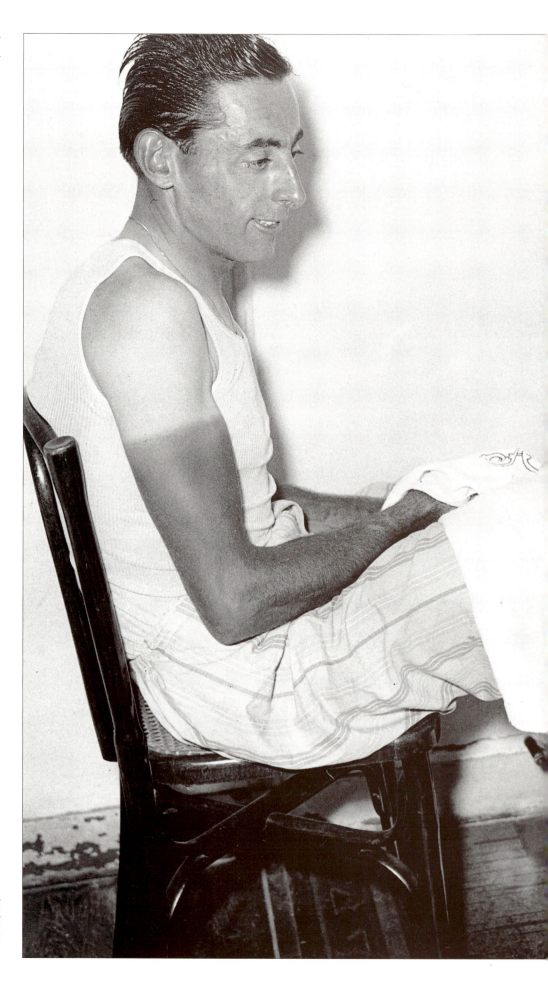

Coppi, his feet in the water. Bartali would wait until he had left his hotel, then he would search it high and low for clues to a miracle product.

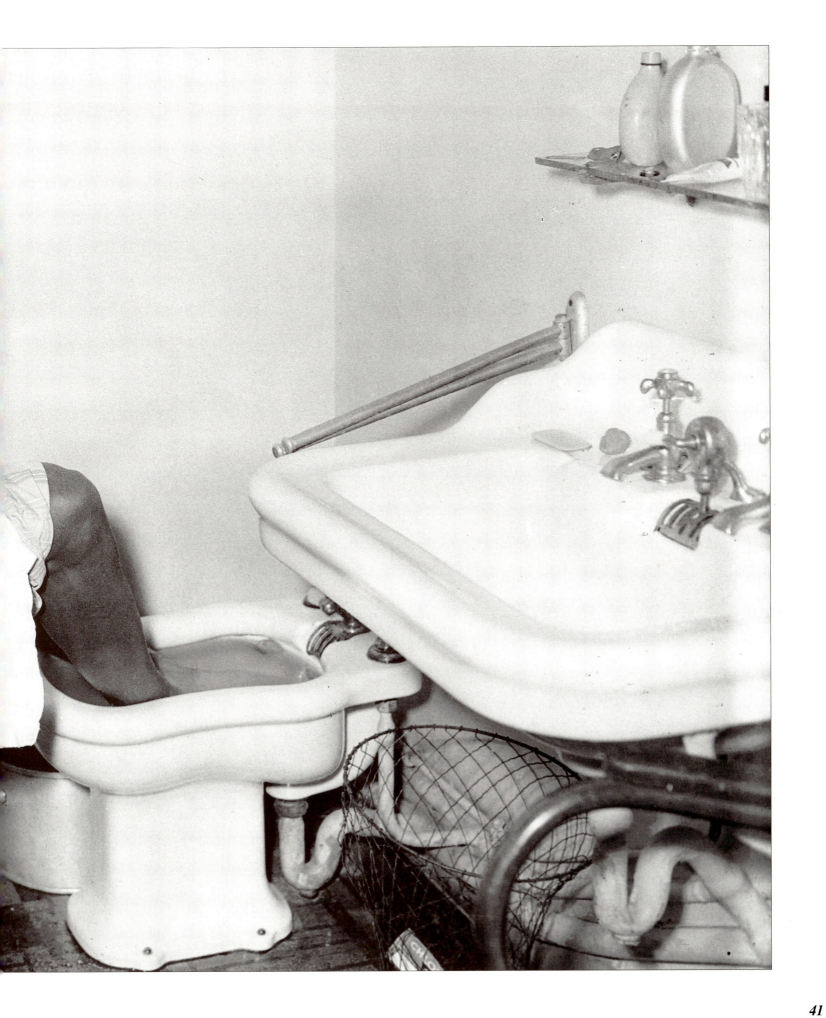

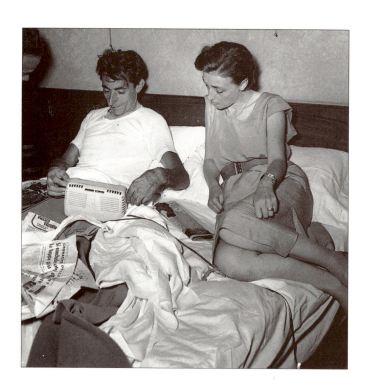

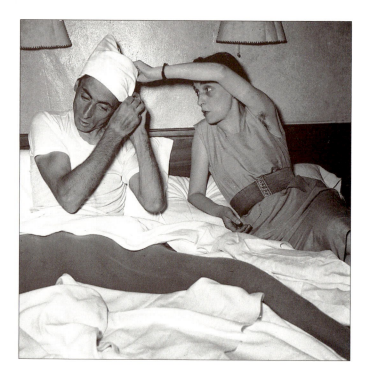

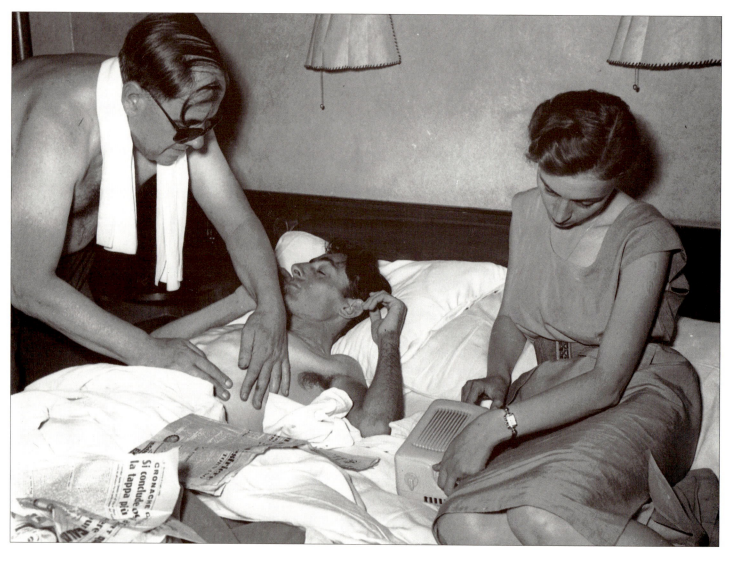

With his first wife, Bruna, in the company of his blind trainer, the famous Cavanna,
Coppi does not yet think of his Dame Blanche.

Half of Italy were behind Bartali, the other half were for Coppi.

He took advantage of a day off from the Tour to enjoy sweets and pastries.

Kubler and Koblet, two opposite styles but a reciprocal esteem.

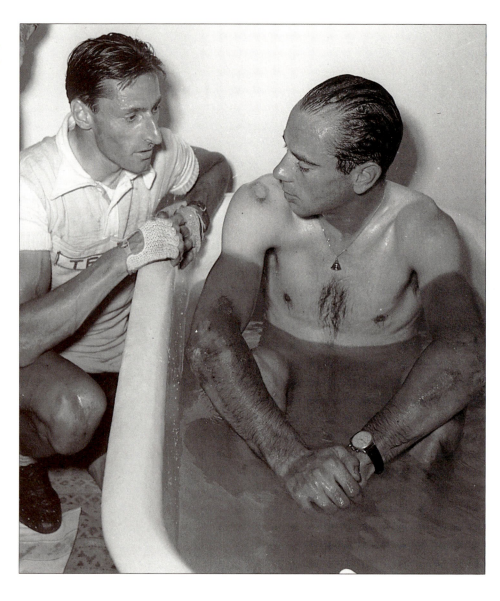

KOBLET & KUBLER

In 1951, while Bartali smoked Nazionales and Coppi mourned the brutal death of his brother Serse, Hugo Koblet began the Tour without ever having been an amateur. The year before he dominated the Giro, leaving the job of bringing back the Tour to his compatriot, Ferdi Kubler.

Switzerland, which did not enjoy as big a cycling tradition as France, Italy or Belgium, was in awe of the success of the "Two Ks", Koblet and Kubler. With an eruptive and violent temper, Kubler had imposed himself with his strong will, to become one of the best racers of his generation. Geminiani warned him against the dangers of Mont Verneux, "Be careful Ferdi, it's not a mountain like any other..." he warned. Kubler answered "Ferdi Kubler is not a racer like any other, Ferdi is a great

champion!" He had always had to assert himself, and now he showed his courage loud and clear. It was his way of exorcising or showing his pain. His style of pedaling was abrupt, compared to that of Hugo Koblet, which was aerial and more dynamicly sound. "Without Kubler, there would never have been a Koblet, and without Koblet, Kubler would not have existed," Kubler said. It was hardly an exaggeration. The "Two K's" formed two distinct species, opposite from one another, yet inseparable in legend.

In 1951, a year of incredible activity, Kubler powered himself in the Ardennais Weekend, (the Fleche Wallone was set for Saturday, and the Liege-Bastogne-Liege was on Sunday) followed by the Tour de Swisse. Koblet won the Tour de France, in spite of Coppi, who was still in mourning and acted

like a stranger to the race, going through the motions as though he was a sleepwalker. In spite of Bobet and Bartali and in spite of all common sense, he forged his success between Briva and Agen, with a sudden solitary disappearance of 135 kilometers. The experts believed that this was for sure the largest personal exploit in the Tour's history.

A picture immortalized that moment. Koblet took time to comb his hair, with his eyes remaining on his wristwatch, which was ticking off the seconds separating him from his pursuers, a total of two minutes and twenty-nine seconds. It was more than a demonstration of athletic prowess, it was an explosion, a leap into eternity.

"If he continues at that rate, the only thing left for me to do is sell my bicycle and change professions!" exclaimed Geminiani, who thought he had seen it all before. It was only after the fact that he found out the real reason for this superhuman act. Koblet was in fact motivated by a strong attack of hemoroids! To keep it a secret, the team technical director did not alert the team's physician, but instead called a private doctor from Brive, whose name he found in the telephone book.

The day after, Koblet decided to attack again, this time for more than 140 kilometers under a sun so hot it melted the tar. He raced alone, hands on the handlebars, without shoulder movement, in his own perfectly sovereign style, distancing himself not only from a group of the "crazy ones", but from the biggest competitors of his generation. And what competitors they were! We found Fausto Coppi, Gino Bartali, Fiorenzo Magni, Raphael Geminani, Louison Bobet, Jean Robic and Stan Ockers, all in agreement that congratulations were due him.

Twelve kilometers from Algen, even though he had the World Championship in his hands, Koblet revealed a surprising vulnerability. "I can't stand it anymore," he told his technical director, "I am going to stop." From the wheel of his car, Alex Burtin inflated Koblet's bicycle tire, and from there he went on to win the Tour and along with it his place in history.

Months later, while in Mexico for the Tour of Mexico, he contracted a veneral disease, which, at that time, was incurable if not treated in time, and this tolled the bell of sublime hope, the beginning of the end or perhaps more correctly, the end of the beginning. The beginning of Koblet's career (nicknamed the "Cyclist of Charm" by the humorist Jacques Grello) had only given a glimpse of his immense talent. Koblet came back twice to the Tour, in 1953 and 1954, and twice he left without glory, offering the public an image of a man torn inside. The man was pushed to the end of his rope,

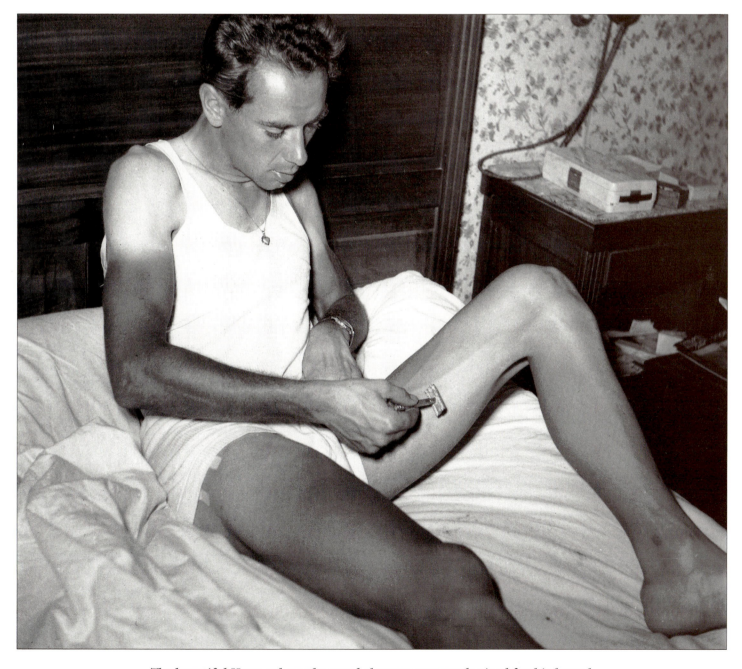

The beautiful Hugo, where the word elegance was predestined for his legend.

and if he ran again in winter in the circuit of the Six Jours, it was only because he had to, because he had a lot of trouble just maintaining his exorbitant lifestyle. He prolonged his activity until 1956, but it was only his ghost who won a lap that year in the Tour of Spain, with the blessings of Rik Van Steenbergen and Miguel Poblet.

A professional failure suffering emotional damage, Koblet no longer knew what to do with his life which ended on November 2, 1964 as a result of a car accident. The day he died, his white Alfa Romeo was traveling more than 120 kilometers an hour when it crashed into a tree on the road which crossed Esslingen town in the direction of Ulster. At the scene of the accident the road was completely dry, and showed no trace of the brakes having been applied. The country was calm and serene. Had he lost control of his car, or had he committed suicide? An investigation for mechanical failure was called off. It would not have shown the real cause of the accident. Before dying, Koblet remained in a coma for four days. That coma affected one-by-one: Magni, Bartali, Bobet and Coppi; all competitor's of his on Algen's road, in 1951, on a beautiful summer day.

To date, only a sincere and intense regret remains. The idea that in cycling there were two kinds of champions: the ones who achieved notoriety with courage were the most numerous, but their memory fades with time; and then those rare ones who cross their time in a unique flash.

Ferdi Kubler was from the first kind, Koblet from the second, but history has enjoyed putting the black devil and the blond angel together in a eulogy full of grace and profound humanity.

He embodied the state of grace, yet he had a propensity to go astray.

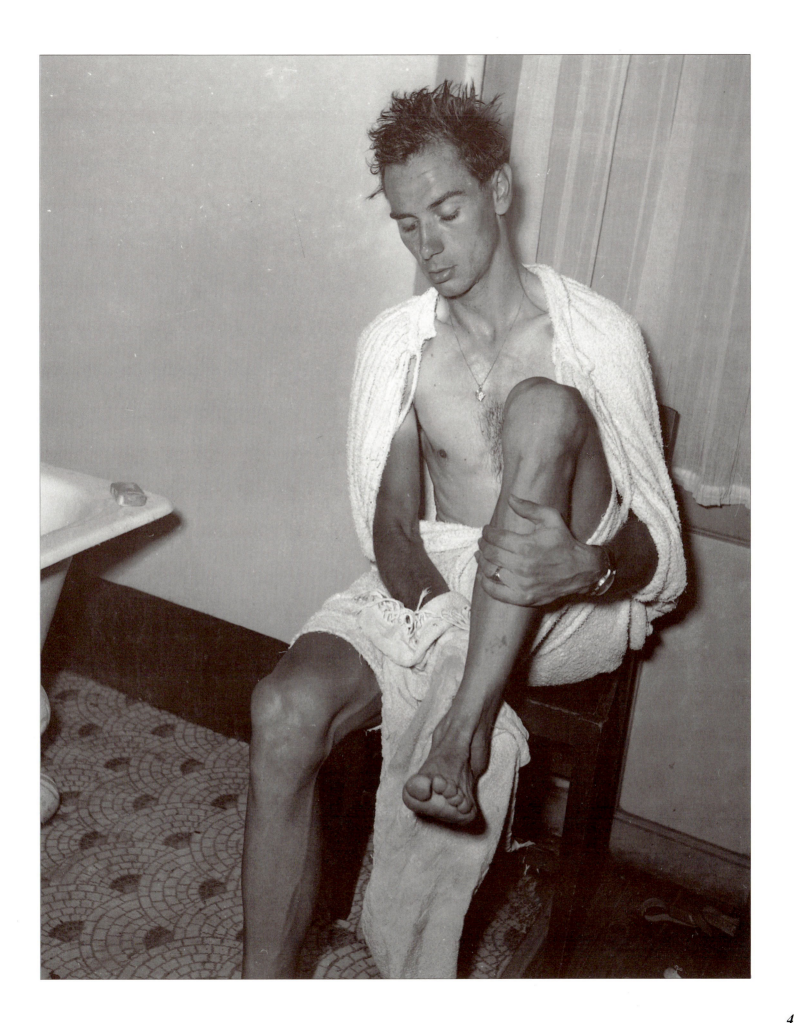

Kubler, in one of his grand cyranesque tirades. The Swiss was sometimes subject to the violent moods. (1949)

Rik Van Steenbergen only made one appearance in the Tour de France, in 1949. He won the stage of Toulouse, but the gain corrupted any ambition the Belgian possessed, which he turned instead to winning classics and the Six Days race. The Tour was too big for him and its mountains too rough.

RIK VAN STEENBERGEN

When his steps took him back to the low quarters of Seefhoek, he became lost in the little island of Eilandje, where the war had driven some really bizarre individuals, adept at the black market. As he absorbed his surroundings, Rik Van Steenbergen was overcome by a curious and uncomfortable feeling. Anver's youth had disappeared. The tall grass, which smothered the dark buildings caused as much damage as enemy bombs had during the war. On the outskirts of the Sportspalais, narrow alleys from nowhere converged to end in an enclosed area, bordered by vacant lands like some deserted memory. Landslides remained within steel pilings in sight of Jeff Meuwiss' bistro, which was frequented by the locals who slept off their drunken stupor behind the steel curtain. Only the pavement sent back the echo of memories under the virgin steps of pedestrians strolling. Beyond the vacant lands, the factories rose up, spewing their black smoke, streaking the feathers of the few white seagulls flying above them. Off in the distance, the town breathed in the fresh ocean air. Sirens screamed about the death of a vanquished world. It had been a very long time since the velodrome bell

had rung it's time for the last race. The Rik of old is himself no longer "King of the Road" where ladies used to greet him with an alluring smile.

He was only 18 years old when in August of 1943 he became Champion of Belgium ahead of the professional George Claes on the Allee Vert (Green Alley) circuit. He was barely twenty years old when he finished ahead of Brik Schotte in the Tour des Flandres. Disemboweled by the sea, Anvers crouched under the bombardment of war, rejecting it's disgust from it's pores of anguish. With the flood of GIs and Marines came the deep voice of Nat King Cole on the radio, plus Frankie Lane and Louis Armstrong. Rik frequented the bars and appreciated the new jukeboxes. The post-war era also had it's upside for him. Despite the scorched soil of Flanders and the neighboring Ardennes, he walked that period of time carrying with him the secret hope that one day he would cross the Atlantic in search of a salvaged and prolific life.

At war's end in 1945, he had no money, but his name had already resounded all over Belgium, from Brussels to Namur, from Anvers to Gand. On the verge of reconstruction and with the audacity of a person in his twenties, he became the

symbol of inert hope of a new generation. He was surrounded by ruins. Bridges were dismantled. Railroads destroyed. The Sportspalais no longer had a roof. To survive, young Steenbergen traveled all over Europe in search of a cycling contract. Often he went to Switzerland, one of the few neighboring countries spared the shortages of war. He always came back richer, arms full of watches, which he rushed to sell at a profit. For Rik Van Steenbergen, son of a laborer (his father rolled cigars by hand at the Maligne factory) there were no savings to fall back on.

Rik Van Steenbergen did not possess the charisma of Jacques Anquetil nor the discreet elegance of Koblet. As far as race day appearances went, he came in far behind Fausto Coppi, the idol of the new Italy. Van Steenbergen was rugged and poorly dressed but his looks were just the look of the times. He had deep and penetrating eyes, and combed back his wavy hair. His smile gave off the look of splendor like those American stars from the movies which were just beginning to be shown in the local theatres. In town there were those who believed they'd seen Rik behind the wheel of a Mercury, and inside it were two racing bicycles, a bicycle saddle plus a water bottle. He was ready to make a fortune, or at least for a little while, head in the direction of fame and glory. Rik polished his image. He had only one goal in his mind: to become famous. He wished to become a sports celebrity so that the economic rebound would favor his own development and prosperity. He did not lack for a trump card, because he shined as much on the road as he did in the adulterated world of the Six Jours (Six Days). Some technicians believed that he could become World Speed Champion if he so had the desire. Had he not beaten big Arie Van Vleit in the distant 100 kilometer American Tour? Antonin Magne let it be known that he (Magne) could have fought for victory in the Tour de France, but he only "fought" once and that was a fight without much conviction. Rik Van Steenbergen placed second in the Giro, behind Magni but in front of Coppi, Kubler

and Koblet. Rik had to smile when they recalled this subject with him.

Rik noted "In 1946, I was the only one able to follow Bartali on the small mountain pass in the Swiss Tour, but by the following winter I had put on a little weight and right away I took to racing all year long without letup. From that point on, I was lost only in the races of many stages."

For more than twenty years he was able to bear his pain with a surprising amount of self control, an art consumed from the race where he adopted an economic style; sitting back very low in the saddle, in the compact style of an artisian bulldog.

The Flemish are a roughhewn, resistant type. Just a couple of hours rest was enough to put him back on his feet. For sure he did not have the style of a Merckx or the manner of a Van Looy but he possessed one of the most impressive "palmares" (list of wins) in history with: three World Championships, two Paris-Roubaix, two Tours des Flandres, two Fleches-Walonne (with a nine year break inbetween), plus Paris-Brussels, Milan-San Remo and no less than thirteen Belgian Championships; in all possible disciplines.

He won always and he won everywhere, even at 'belotte' (a card game), where he was able to draw in Rene Vitto, who did not know that the Belgian thrived on the game.

Marked forever by the war and its deprivations, he dreamed of being able to offer his wife Maria and their five children the comfort and education that he had never had. In his hectic, busy life he thought only about money. He constantly criss-crossed Europe pocketing slim profits, going sleepless behind the wheel of his car. He raced day and night, summer and winter, ate lunch on the run and slept with one eye open looking for the detour sign at the village entrance. He showed up everywhere his presence was demanded, travelling alone, wearing odd-looking jerseys and constantly keeping track of his expenses. In Paris, Van Steenbergen preferred to eat a sandwich under the Bir-Hakeim subway station rather than dine at Routis with Fausto Coppi, Louison Bobet

or Gerrit Schulter. Two hours prior to Paris-Roubaix he was content to eat just one hard-boiled egg. For him, one pair of socks was enough for the season, and when those socks had holes in them, he raced without them in just his leather shoes.

Over a quarter century, he covered two million kilometers, equal to thirty-eight times around the world, and at a time when travel was tiring with congested roads and uncomfortable trains. In 1957 he established a record of sorts where, for him, it was not uncommon to be in Leopoldville on July 16, in Copenhagen the day after, then in Roncourt, followed by Paris the next day. The extraordinary fact of all this was, he ended up a winner every time. He was homesick for sure and very sad. Some days he resented this unreasonable life he had chosen, but he calmed himself down, since he suffered from the neurosis that he lived an unreal life. With his first salary, he built an apartment building. Thereafter he owned five, one for each of his children.

Assisted by his fame, he was thought to be untouchable while driving, because when he violated a traffic sign, police officers always let him go without a citation.

All the gates fell before him until one day he began sensing his own decline and began looking for a new reason to believe in the future. That was when Rik had to confront some difficult times. At the beginning of his career, he could count on the paternal friendship of Karel Kaers and the advice of Antonin Magne, known for his wisdom, which had guided Rik to his fertile and lucrative success. Now he found himself on a road without lanes, dispossessed from his role, constrained to find some new anchor points in his life, because on his bicycle he could feel old age creeping into his legs. Van Steenbergen had only one vice: GAMBLING. It gave him a sense of freedom, a feeling of extreme ecstasy. Van Steenbergen worked hard for his money, facing the likes of Anquetil, Coppi and Van Looy, but he willingly threw away that hard earned money on the "carpet" of the gaming table. "I never understood him," Fred de

Jean Robic and Raoul Remy share a bath during the Tour.

Bruyne said, "Rik was tight with money like no one I've ever seen, to the point of cutting one franc in two, but he would gamble his fortune on one ace of spades." He took this bad habit with him everywhere he went. He frequented all the gambling circles of Anvers. In the Port Quarter, there were persons of unsavory moral character, always coming to him wanting to play cards, but the games were fixed with marked cards and subtle signals etc. Those people stripped him of his fortune. To come back he was reduced to doing hazardous traffic at the Dutch border. Not really big things but delivering packages, the contents of which he ignored, along with the name of the recipient. At least that is what he told the Customs Agent who waited for him at the Rosiere in the Brabant Wallon. Did Rik identify himself as the mythical person Raoul Walsh or Frank Capra, men who had fascinated him in his youth? Was he a victim of entrapment? Was it just an error? By carrying all that excess baggage, he reverted to the labyrinth of his childhood. It was his mother who had given him the keys. "She was born in a bar and had a passion for poker," Rik said. "It was she who passed the virus on to me." Mr. Van der Poorten, the Minister of Justice used all of his status and power and gave Van Steenbergen only a couple of days in jail.

It was a shattered man who for the last time came back in the autumn of 1966 on the hardwood floor of the Anvers Sportpalais and just broke down.

LOUISON BOBET

The aristocrat of the cycling world, he carried a certain social pretention. Louison Bobet, here in 1959, welcomed his defeat with a profound humiliation.

The Izoard in 1954: Bobet in his solitary exercise of power.

Under the eyes of Bartali, sick and demoralized, he says goodbye to the Tour de France at the summit of the Iseran.

First abandon in 1949. An unexpected determination can be read in the face of the Breton. We will speak again of him.

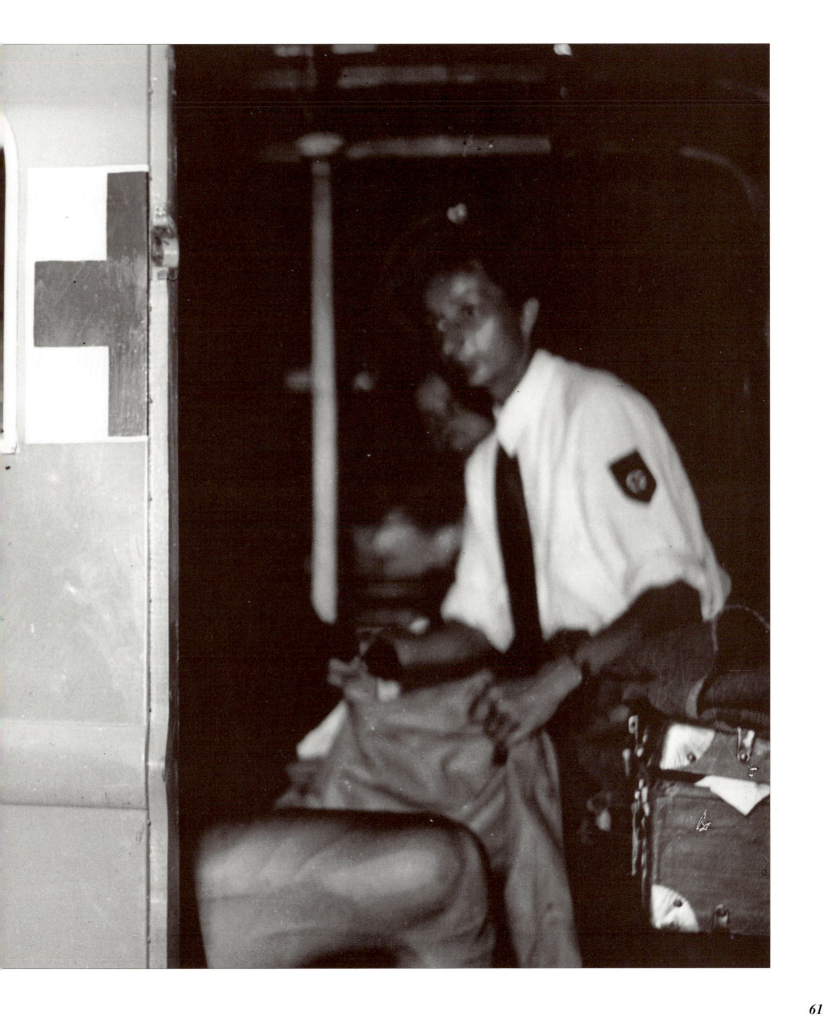

Anquetil in the reflection of his celebrity.

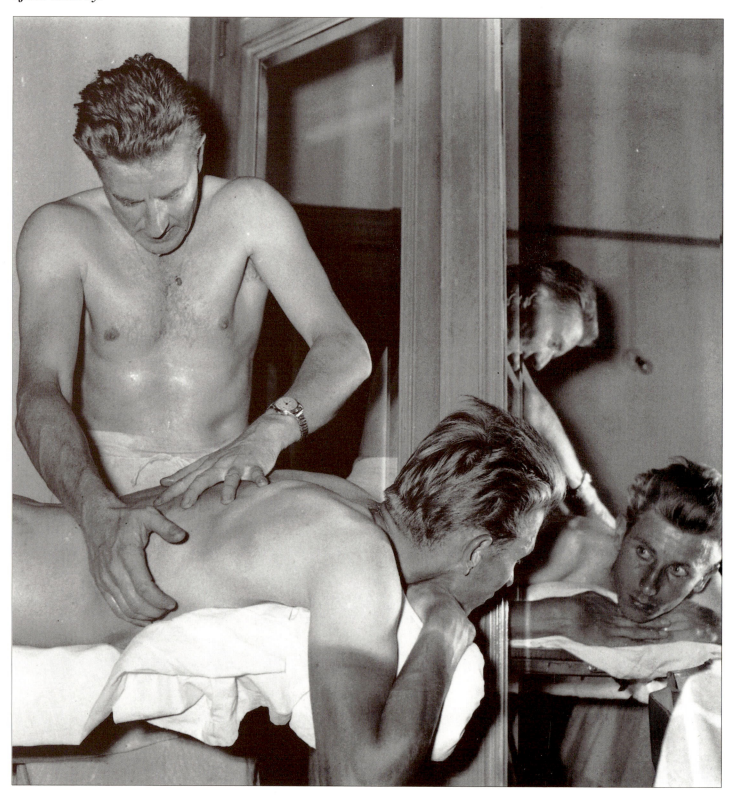

JACQUES ANQUETIL

When he retired from the sport scene in December, 1969, the French people discovered, with amazement, that this exceptional champion, the one to whom they gave only measured sympathy, had occupied a place in the press equal to Sartre, Bardot, or Sagan.

Winner at age 17 of the Grand Prix des Nations, and bringing home the Barrachi's trophy at age 34, Felice Gimondi's partner, Jacques Anquetil, was able to push aside the age distance and weave a rapport among several generations of cyclists. Coppi's generation had introduced him to modern cycling, and Merckx's generation was presumed to be his successor. In the seventeen years of his career, he had won five Tours de France, two Tours d'Italie, the Bordeaux-Paris race, plus the Grand Prix des Nation nine times. In 1956, during

his military service, he attacked Fausto Coppi's mystic record by covering 46.159 kilometers in one hour. It was the same record that he would beat eleven years later on Vigorelli's trail and little did he care inside that he had not been endorsed. This champion did not live his life at the expense of others. He maintained an almost obsessional rapport with time. At the wheel of his car, he took pleasure beating a speed record between Rouen and Paris by driving all night without lights while the highway was deserted. He could predict the length of time a trip would take down to the second.

Since his father had shown him the deactivation of a mine on the beach at Normandy, Anquetil took pleasure in provoking destiny; like driving on roads with no lanes just for an escape. No matter what season it was, he ate and drank to his

heart's content. He preferred to eat seafood and would rather trim his sleep in order to satisfy his passion for poker or gin-rummy. He ignored all the Parisian snobishness and existential lifestyle but without realizing it he also copied it. He loved nights of drinking and the pale ghostly mornings at Neuville-Chant d'Oisell where he had purchased Maupassant's old home. Old-timers predicted a phenomenal career for him. Once, while seeing him gulp down a lobster covered with mayonnaise, soaked in white wine before the beginning of a race, Apo Lazarides concluded with a hearty, prophetic laugh, "he may be making his debut in cycling, but the end is near".

Louison Bobet agreed with this opinion. The press couldn't help themselves and constantly underlined all his escapades, his constant shifting from one

Jacques and Janine: he was her champion, she was his muse, his faithful companion.

thing to another, his uncertain lifestyle which appeared strange even for a bicycle racer. He preferred drinking whiskey to fruit juice. Spending evenings with friends who kept him awake until morning did not stop him from accepting all the challenges offered by Raymond Poulidor, Rik Van Looy, or Federico Bahamontes, who were dumbfounded by this amusing person, this super human phenomenon. Jacques Anquetil was looking to reconcile his life with his job, and without a doubt this was something his life truly needed. He was a healthy monster and one that the medical staff found disconcerting. Dr Andrivet, who had seen him spitting blood during the 1958 Tour de France and six months later being a live wire in the Grand Prix des Nations race, said of him, "he possesses the most voluminous heart of anyone in French sports".

Legend held together the privileged, implacable image of a champion. Anquetil proved to be a metronome against the stopwatch, but he suffered like the others and knew defeats as well as rewards. In the 1958 Tour de France, he collapsed in the Chartruese, a victim of congestion. Then in 1962 in the Vuelta, he secretly vomited, hiding his weakness from his teammates. That same year, at the Baracchi, Rudi Altig humiliated him in front of the tifosi crowd. Jean Bobet said, "on the straight roads leading to Bergame, I saw Anquetil pedaling flat out for 50 kilometers. He saw nothing and heard nothing, but he followed Louison Bobet". Did he follow at 50 kilometers an hour? The misfortune happened as he entered the Bergame podium. A sharp turn appeared

on the left. Anquetil went straight ahead into the crowd, a couple of meters after crossing the finish line.

There was also the famous episode of Mechoui Andorre in the 1964 Tour de France. His failure in the uphill portion of Envelira, where he held on like a man possessed, for more than four minutes behind the tandem of Bahamontes and Poulidor. At the departure for Rennes "Beline the Magi" predicted his death during the fourteenth stage of the race. After that time Jacques lived under constant pressure. After the "Magi's" articles came threatening letters.

"I don't want to die riding a bicycle" repeated Jacques, "I prefer to give up".

He lived a real life drama and often could not sleep at night. In an attempt to distract himself on his days off, he listened to a mix of music put together by a radio station. In one picture we see him looking satisfied as he ate lamb only to find out later he had only tasted the lamb to please the photographers. On the following day (the prophetic day) it wasn't from indigestion but from a scare out of the blue that paralyzed him on the Envelira summit, where Ralph Geminiani was able to get him out of his torpor by telling him, "Jacques you are five minutes forty seconds behind Bahamontes and Poulidor, so if you want to die, please don't die in front of the broom wagon".

The legend of Jacques Anquetil is not complete without speaking of the young lady who accompanied him, night and day, mixing her blond personna with the reflection of his glory. Her name was Janine. She was the wife of his physician,

and she had a strong influence on Anquetil and his career. When you have to race more than one hundred days a year, and you are risking your life on the downhill, taking in all kinds of vitamins just to stay alive, your equilibrium is affected. Jacques, like other racers, lived on the edge, but Janine was always there for him, showing her affection. She did not hesitate to cut across France at the wheel of his Opel to join him or to drive him from one Criterium to another, while Jacques remained sleeping in the back seat completely exhausted. It took only a whisper from his voice showing a little worry and she would be right there, and happy to be there. She was simply content that he was happy in her presence. For many years, Janine was everything to him, confidante, nurse and chauffeur. Jacques and Janine. Janine and Jacques. They were everything to each other. Each was nothing without the other. Their names entwined and their mixed initials took on the world that witnessed their tumultuous affair. They made quite a pair. She was close to him like Elsa Triolet was to Aragon, like Piaf for Cerdan or Signoret for Montand. She was a mistress, loving and passionate, whose fatal beauty radiated in the shadow of the champion. Those who tried to follow on their crazy escapades invariably had to turn back. There was no place for others with these two incorrigible and malicious lovers. They were proud to be together and show their happiness in broad daylight in spite of the prejudices of the time. They shared an audacious freedom following their bewildering announcement in the spring of 1968. For Anquetil, Janine left her husband and her son (who later joined her), attracted by an unbridled life she leaped and landed with both feet planted firmly beside the young, popular

and triumphant champion.

Her intrusion into the ultra-conservative circle of championship cycling stirred up jealousy and vindication. She was the prey of those who saw her only as a complicated yet happy show off. In the presence of Jacque's professional entourage, Janine often felt on the outside looking in. She stood tall with dignity, as women who are caught up in adversity are capable of doing. She stayed close to Jacques, always being his "Dame Blanche" (white lady), without worrying about what was being said about her. To those who preferred that Anquetil disassociate his love life from his job he sharply responded that "to prepare for a race there is nothing better than a good pheasant, some champagne and a woman". He was joking of course, because he was unable to find any other words to describe his fascination with Janine. Struck by her beauty, he found that he was unable to resist her. She was sexy and feminine, with a mischievous look similar to Martine Carol, the actress. Her platinum hair captured the rays of the sun. Sure of her seductive charm, she followed fashion, manners and the spirit of that time with an easy-going grace.

Jacques had already been victorious in the Grand Prix des Nations race and all of France held on to him and his prodigy. He met her in the office of Dr. Boeda, who was Janine's husband. Janine, the accomplished wife, was the person who scheduled the Doctor's appointments. They met again in February of 1957. On the way to Genes, they made a date for dinner that same evening at a restaurant in Villefranche, where she was going on vacation. After that evening they were never apart. After each racing victory they celebrated their union.

Jacques Anquetil was born January 8, 1934 in Mont-St.-Aignant to a family of strawberry growers. There was little mention made of his father, other than he was, apparently, an untreated alcoholic whose addiction may have been brought on by his occupation. As for his mother, tired of her husband's drinking, she left the family and had only the briefest of contact with her son. Years later she showed up one evening at Val d'Hiver stadium to acclaim the son she brought into the world, and whom the world was just beginning to know. At age 17, Anquetil joined the ranks of the cycling team AC Sotteville. There he met a renowned technician by the name of Andre Boucher, who detected in that rosy-cheeked, good-looking country boy, a rare talent for besting the stopwatch, and who showed the promise of a grand future. As the saying goes, "the teacher had met his student".

"I hold in my hand a born cyclist, whose actions make me think of the movements of a clock," said Andre Boucher of Jacques Anquetil. The trainer guided him with a firm hand and Anquetil forged for himself an iron will. At 17, while preparing for the French Amateur Championship at Carcassone, which he would win, he caught the eye of Francis Pelissier, whose nickname was "the Sorcerer". Pelissier was the person who involved Anquetil in the Grand Prix des Nations race, a race of 140 kilometers held in the Chevreuse Valley. This was the beginning of a fabulous destiny. Anquetil made an awesome entry, pulling away from the Creton by 7 kilometers. The Norman aesthetic caught the eye of all the "horse traders" of the cycling world, who were caught up by the purity of his style. They all wanted him on their team. Antonin

Magne courted him in his style which was frank and polite, but in the end it was Francis Pelissier who was the high bidder.

Anquetil rejoined Koblet at the Perle, but his harmony with Pelissier was short-lived, because the latter committed a serious breach of diplomacy. In 1954 Pelissier chose to patronize a Swiss racer in the Grand Prix des Nations thus indicating a preference and obviously bruising the ego of Anquetil. So it was with a feeling of vexation that the Norman, assisted by a good mechanic, won at the Parc des Princes, where Koblet's defeat was compounded by Francois Pelissier's error.

Anquetil's career was now flying, but the Pelissier episode had opened his eyes to how merciless the professionals in cycling could be. He now knew that his success, if there was to be any, would come from a solitary adventure. His precocity condemned him to be the prey of his rivals, because it is impossible to possess both youth and great talent without arousing jealousy in others. He inherited from his parents the philosophy that nothing is gained without effort, and to take nothing for granted, and that all pain will be rewarded. He was exigent with his salary and this practice drove him to neglect the classic races in favor of the more profitable Tour de France, where the stars reinforced their fame and notoriety.

His plan was simple. He was content to put down his competitors in the chronometered sections of a race and then follow them on the mountains, preferring to endure rather than shine. He won five Tours de France, but each victory was received by a sullen public, which found him too irrational. Even Jacques Goddet went on to call him the "yellow dwarf" (as opposed to a "giant of the road"). It would be redundant to say that the Norman took this comment badly and it caused a rift between them.

Anquetil did not possess Koblet's halo, nor Coppi's spirit, which was capable of burning an opponent with a single acceleration. He also lacked the devouring ambition which animated Eddy Merckx. However, Anquetil distanced himself from his rivals and became, according to Antoine Blondin, "the first functional champion in history". The new world of championship

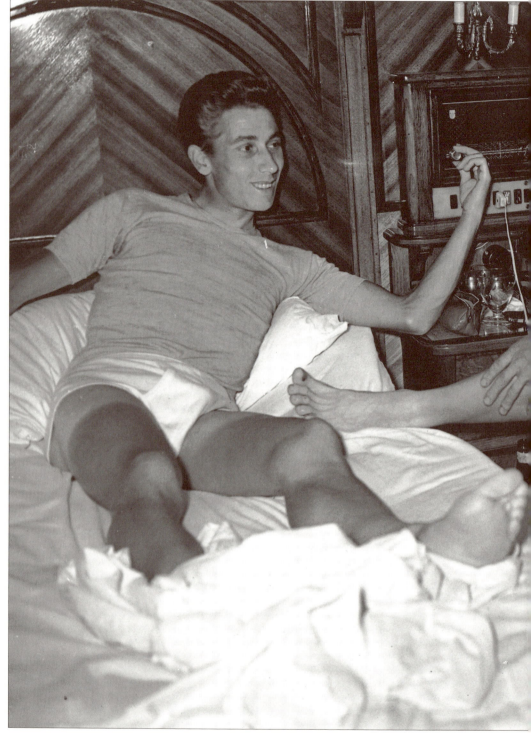

A solid friendship existed with Andre Darrigade and Jean Forestier, two other pilars

cycling came with extra "sportif" brands and now was a sport with commercialism and a businessman's sense of logic. Louison Bobet represented the French nationalism of the "after-the-war" mentality with the tri-color teams. Conversely, Anquetil was his own career manager. Prior to him, France had cried in the face of Rene Vitto's sacri-fice and then there was Roger Riviere's crashing spectacle at the bottom of the Perjuret. In him, France was able to wean herself away from crying over past tragedies. Anquetil imposed himself on the cycling world and always took the breath away from those who saw him race. Faithful to his own philosophy, he defend-

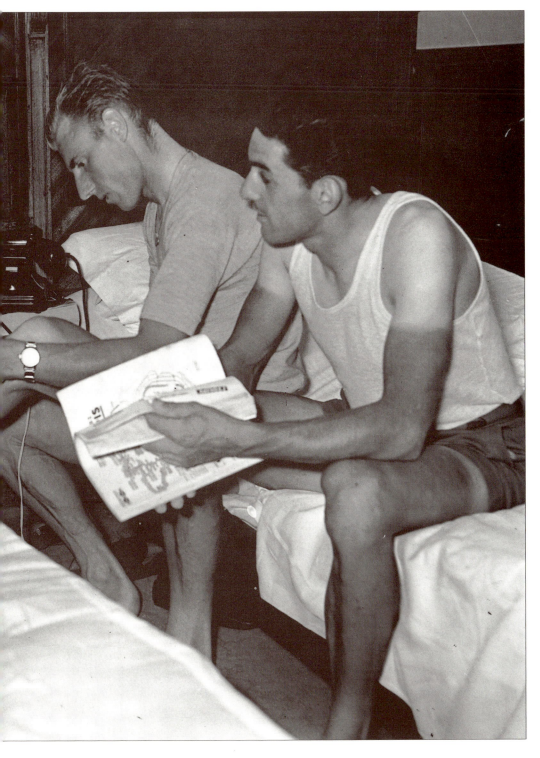

of the French team.

knocked him out of the victory slot just twelve kilometers shy of the finish line, which was won by the Belgian Van Daele. This incident comforted him in his conviction that he had more to lose than win in the classics. "There were no races, only lotteries," grumbled the Norman. France had to be patient until 1964 when he pressed himself to win the Grand-Wevelgem, and two years later to see him add the Liege-Bastogne-Liege Tour to his prestigious "palmares" (list of wins). He already linked his career with that of Ralphael Geminiani, who was the ex-partner of Fausto Coppi at Bianchi and Louison Bobet under the French team jersey. He appreciated the dynamics, the proficient techniques and diplomacy of the French team. Geminiani liked Jacques for his athletic prowess, his strong will and his defiance, which was tightly linked to his love for the sport. Geminiani knew how to manipulate this champion, exploit his romanticism and stimulate his pride at any given opportunity. "Anquetil is like a reactor and a computer," Geminiani remarked. No one had ever given a better definition of the champion.

In 1965 the Norman took a chance by not racing in the Tour, feeling that a sixth victory would not really enhance his market value. Geminiani made him understand the necessity to reaffirm his prestige. This came in the double Dauphine-Bordeaux-Paris race. Two years later it is Geminiani once again who convinces Anquetil to make another run at the record time. He breaks it with a new record time of 43.493 kilometeres in one hour. He had sworn before that he would never attempt it again.

Anquetil was never able to sway public opinion to his side, perhaps because he viewed cycling as a need rather than a goal. He suffered in silence that they preferred Poulidor and that they focused popular passions on Raymond Poulidor, with his healthy, country-boy demeanor.

For two decades these two men opposed each other violently. Their confrontation became particularly sharp in 1964 on the Puy-de-Dome uphill, where the Norman, tired from his recently completed Tour d'Italy (which he won) had all he could do to contain the spirit of the

ed his own interests, concerned more about preserving his place as the leading money winner. He favored the Federico Bahamontes version of success to that of Henri Anglade in 1959. In 1967 Anquetil reproached his teammates: Riotte, Stablinski and Lemetayer for their profering his services to Roger Pingeon and Raymond

Poulidor under the tri-color jersey.

He made only one infraction to the code of conduct that he recalled. This was in 1958, when he was leading in the Paris-Roubaix and expected to win. He had prepared himself like a demon, doubling his training intensity. However, the victory he expected eluded him when a flat tire

An historic moment: suffering from congestion, Anquetil descends from his bicycle in the cote de Serriere, in the territory of the Ardeche. He abandonned the Tour and would not return again.

Anquetil did not know his grand popularity. He would not be subjected again to the damages of the route. He retired with the sentiment of having been the least liked and the most admired.

Limousan. Their duel, well orchestrated by the press, rested in their opposing styles; one appearing to be the innocent victim (Poulidor), and the other a relentless persecutor (Anquetil). In his favor, the French partisan crowd of the '60s showed a clear inclination towards the Limousan (Poulidor), whom they had nicknamed "Poupou". For the Norman, they reserved their harshest criticism, even sometimes revelling in his defeats. In his defense, Anquetil kept to himself. Those around him saw in him a very profound disenchantment. It was this disenchantment, which inspired him during the 1967 Tour de France. In a week of sensational newspaper headlines, with crashing revelations on the morals of cycling, he put Poulidor back in his place by declaring that he was "on drugs" and further that "everyone was doing it". This remark was considered very couragious for a champion of his rank to make. Anquetil reiterated it months later in front of Francois Missoffe, the French Minister of Youth and Sports, stating further: "How would you like to race Bordeaux-Paris with mineral water. You begin by taking a sugar cube, then coffee, then some chocolate and from then on it's like a frenzy. You are drugged!" To Francoise Giroud, who questioned him about this remark, he answered: "In the jungle, small trees never grow."

Anquetil had literally a horror of convention. He acted like a free man, never worrying if he shocked public opinion, because his statement permitted him the ability to cross over from his profession. He

attracted sympathy from numerous intellectuals. He even received the Legion of Honor medal from Charles de Gaulle.

During the last two years of his reign, chipped at by the arrival of Eddie Merckx, he was able to reconcile his professional activities with the expansion of his agricultural domain. He retired in November, 1969, after a reunion on the Charleroi Velodrome. His new life as an agricultural manager fascinated him. He imported cows from Wyoming and devoted himself to the cultivation of grains. He followed the Tour for the publication Europe 1 and managed the French Team to the World Championships. In the early 1980s his health began to deteriorate and he became haunted by thoughts of death. First he had a pulmonary congestion in 1976. This was followed by a relapse two years later, when he believed he was dying of suffocation. These setbacks made him realize that the sands of time do in fact run out too soon. He began to live until he became overcome with exhaustion and he passed his nights observing the wild boars racing about in the Volgboel woods near his home. He was so afraid to sleep fearing he would not wake up, that he practically never slept, revealed a close friend. One day in May, 1987 came the terrible news that Anquetil was stricken with stomach cancer. It had spread and it appeared that he did not have much time left. Against the advice of his doctors, he decided to once more follow the Tour de France to fulfill obligations previously made by providing updates on the Tour and also to report the

date of his forthcoming operation.

On August 11, surgeons from the Central Hospital of Rouen removed his stomach and prescribed for him a draconian diet. However, once released from the hospital, he resumed living his life much like he always had. He approached his illness with detachment, applying to his daily life the courage and lucidity that had animated him during his cycling career. At St. Hilaire Clinic in Rouen, where he was admitted after a relapse, he assembled the last of his strength to receive his close friends for a final farewell. Facing Raymond Poulidor, with whom he had become the closest of friends (time had erased old wounds), he said briefly: "Sorry Raymond...but once again you will finish second". To Andre Darrigarde he said: "I did think ahead ... I have just taken care of my own business." He was referring to his by-then complicated love life. The next day, on November 18, 1987 a great champion left us.

In his *Paris-Match* column, Jacques Goddet came back on the criticism he and numerous other reporters formerly wrote about Anquetil by writing "Were we too harsh on him?" And it was an honest question. The public, reporters, organizers and all others who had formed public opinion of him had to ask themselves 'had they loved him like he had wished to be loved?'

One thing is sure, Jacques Anquetil was the true incarnation of a man who one rarely encounters in life.

Yoga served to relax his muscular body.

RUDI ALTIG

There was Karl Heinz Kunde, the Cologne climber nicknamed "Yellow Dwarf" because of his size, for whom Tour organizers had had to order in a hurry a sport jersey to his size when he became the Tour's leader in 1966. On the opposite side, there was Rudi Altig, "Manheim Colossus", whose true natural strength and muscular body would have been marveled at in a carnival. A high-ranking athlete, he began his race by practicing yoga between two racing matches. In 1960 and 1962, he was a world champion in specialized races, he excelled on the road where his brutal nature was badly accommodated by tactical considerations. A member of the San Raphael Team, he inspired fear in Jacques Anquetil when he dominated him in the Vuelta Race in 1962, after beating him in San Sebastien for the time record.

"Jacques was so upset that he asked me to make Altig race on an ordinary bicycle, after I had used all my influence to make Altig a bicycle he could benefit from, something lighter and with adequate brakes," Raphael Geminiani would reveal, some years later in a photo album.

The German had humiliated the French, in the race for the Baracchi's trophy, by pushing him, ostensibly with an arm, in front of the TV cameras. Then "Master Jacques", revigorated, gave him back a similar test, but this time at Baden-Baden, in front of the German crowd, and strangely enough, they became friends from the moment they stopped being competitors. Altig became Gianni Motta, a big Felice Gimondi, making him the object of an attractive commercial bid. Winner of the Tour des Flanders in 1964 and of San Remo in 1968, he became world champion in front of Anquetil and Poulidor. On the Nurburgring Circuit in 1966, thanks to the deliberate support of Lucien Amor, for "services rendered" in the Tour de France two years earlier.

The well-known Wagnerian was as much at ease in the grand Tours as in the Six Day circles where he teamed up with Kemper, Bugdhal, Renz or Sercu.

Rudi Altig sang his swan song in the 1969 Tour de France where he was the last who could escort Eddy Merckx in the Alsace uphill climbs. Out of luck, the Belgian had chosen that day to strengthen his supremacy on the group. The world of Eurovision saw Altig collapse near the top of the summit, his heart at the edge of implosion, dumbfounded by the phenomenal power of the Belgian champion. His collapse was clean and without dramatics.

He signified the end of a certain romanticism. When he retired in the Bade-Wurtemberg, it had been thirteen years that the press had mixed the echo of his bohemian life with that of the moniacal cycling races; thirteen years that his life was held together by a simple cardboard box, thirteen years of participating in a hazardous business.

The enigmatic Charly Gaul: he mixed his personal torments with those of the Tour de France.

CHARLY GAUL

The reporters nicknamed him "Angel of the Mountain" because he appeared when people least expected him; in the snow flurries of Monte Bondone where he won the 1956 Giro Tour in the fourteen kilometer uphill climb; in the big race of the 1958 Chartreuse Tour performed under an apocalyptic sky. That day Charly Gaul fled into the Luitel and crossed alone over the mountain passes of Porte, Cucheron and Granier, tearing through the curtains of rain, his wool jersey soaked. At the finish line he was fifteen minutes ahead of Geminiani and twenty minutes ahead of Bobet. Anquetil was sick and spitting up blood.

A specialist of the "reversed situation", the Luxembourgian preferred icy rain to strong heat and could prove demonic or at the very least insubordinate with the slightest provocation. He lived to the rhythm of his bad humor and bad attitude.

Trapped by Louison Bobet in the 1957 Giro, while in the midst of a call from nature, Bobet had warned him "I'm going to break your face," so in a spirit of revenge Gaul won the Tour de France in 1958. But this summit champion was associated with the lower ranks of people.

Ninth in the 1962 Tour, he gave up the following year. Then the memory of Charly Gaul became deluted. He tried an unsuccessful comeback in 1964, then retired to a forest in Luxembourg, where he lived like a hermit in a world of rejection, before reappearing obese, and with a long beard and unrecognizeable, as if he were denying his past image, when he was the mountain's "little prince", beardless and sad, and when just a little rain was sufficient to turn into beautiful weather.

RIK VAN LOOY

Who was Rik Van Looy? This question, pondered many times, continues to resonate in the Anvers countryside, the hollow pathway found north of hell (Roubaix), close to Phalampin and Mons-en-Pevele. The question occupies all who knew him from before his time in the limelight to the present. He served as the intermediate bridge between the cycling eras of Rik Van Steenbergen and Eddy Merckx. Less eclectic than the first and less complete than the second, the Flemish allied style with power, mixing in a certain amount of class with his natural and brutal strength. "Van Looy always had a perfumed handkerchief in his jersey back pocket. He need only to breathe in the scent of it and traces would waft back to us as his way of letting us know he was in front," reported an old competitor.

With his milky white complexion, stocky build, and the air of an albatross, the Campinian had the beauty of a Rubens when he raced. When he began his professional career in 1953, he was not yet an electrifying athlete, but he had those weight-lifter thighs combined with pride which would allow him to dominate the classics like no other champion before him. The young Van Looy showed fantastic promise but he was still a dabbler, not yet aware of his strength. At the time his main ambition was to win on his own, when Rik Van Steenbergen first noticed him at Brasschaat's Criterium.

"The young guy with the big thighs, who is he?" the champion asked Stan Ockers. Van Steenbergen had discovered a future virtuoso, trained by the strict Kermesse school and one whose passing bell would soon toll for their own hopes.

At the Bruxelles-Nord train station, at Felicien Vervaeke's cafe near Laeken Castle, finally at Omnium under the pale neon lights of the Anvers Sportspalais, where managers loudly talked their business, encouraged in their trade by the coming of TV coupled with the massive arrival of sports-intensive companys; the talk was only about Fausto Coppi. He was the apostle of modern cycling, always well-dressed and well-groomed, plus he had the logistic support similar to Bianchi, the Italian, who was surrounded by the best race support team of that time. When his prestige was on the line, Coppi didn't hesitate to recruit mercenaries like Prospere De Prodhomme and Desire Keteleer, who joined him in Milan where they had a secret mission to escort the champion in the Primavera at the feet of Turchino. After that they were told to go directly home, without even crossing the finish line.

To break the domination of Van Steenbergen, who was backed by all the networks of interest and occult alliances in the heart of the LVB (Belgium Bicycle League), Rik Van Looy had to turn their idealogy to his own way of thinking. "Van Looy was inspired by Coppi, because he understood from his rivalry with Van Steenbergen that one man alone just did not have enough power and it was therefore necessary to forge alliances with those who would stay by his side in order to win the classics," Brik Schotte noted.

At Team Faema, Van Looy formed his popular "Red Guards". He recruited first-class racers like: Willy Schroeder, Jeff Planckaert, Armand and Gilbert Desmet, Guillaume Van Tongerloo, etc; plus some "kamikazees": Edgar Sorgeloos, Ward Sels,

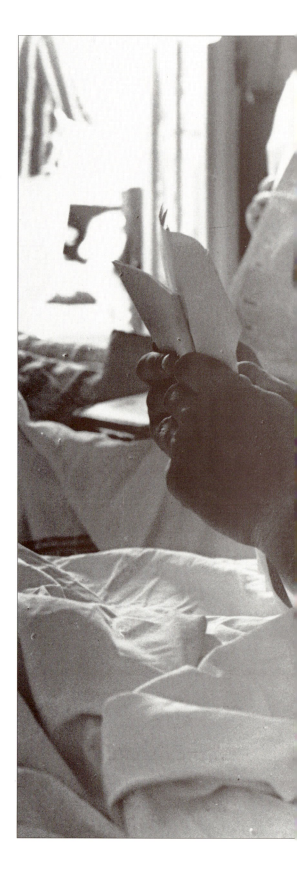

The night would see Van Looy absorbed in the writings of the flemish newspapers, which spoke to him of him.

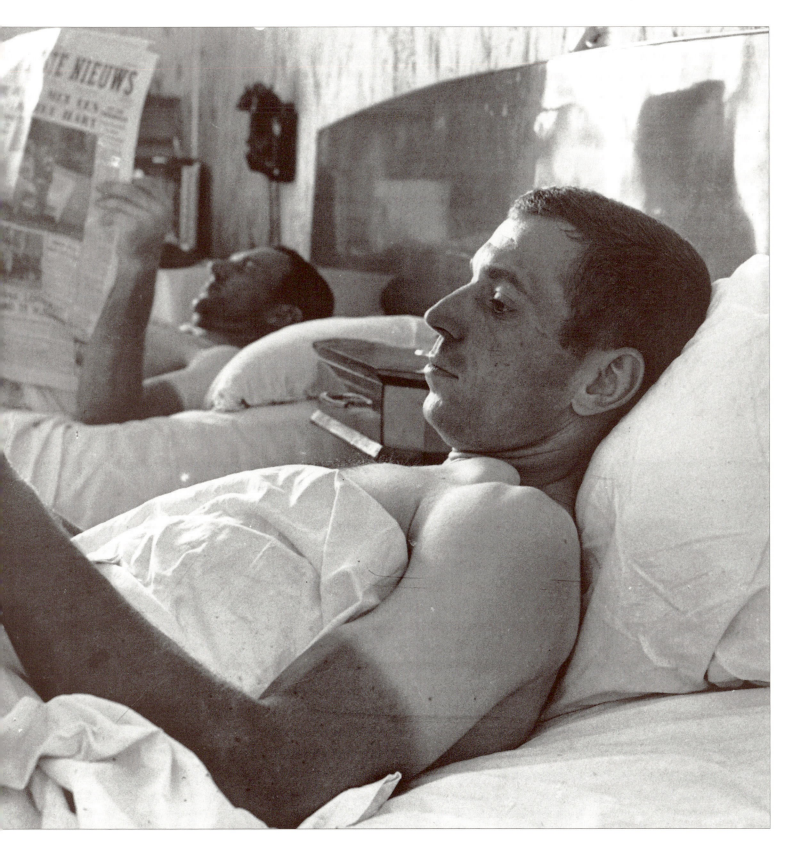

Willy Derboeven, Julien Stevens and Arthur De Cabooter, who were capable of switching off with him during massive sprints. He assured them big bonuses, knowing that money would be the tool to cement their agreement. Soon there were no more seasons because Van Looy pedaled every day. In winter he escaped the fog of Flanders and believed that the warmth of the Riviera would be just too soft for one who wants to compete with the frostiness of Ronde. With his troops he settled in at the Gardonne Barbano Hotel, escorted by a blind trainer. Their days were connected to the changeless rhythm that only he was

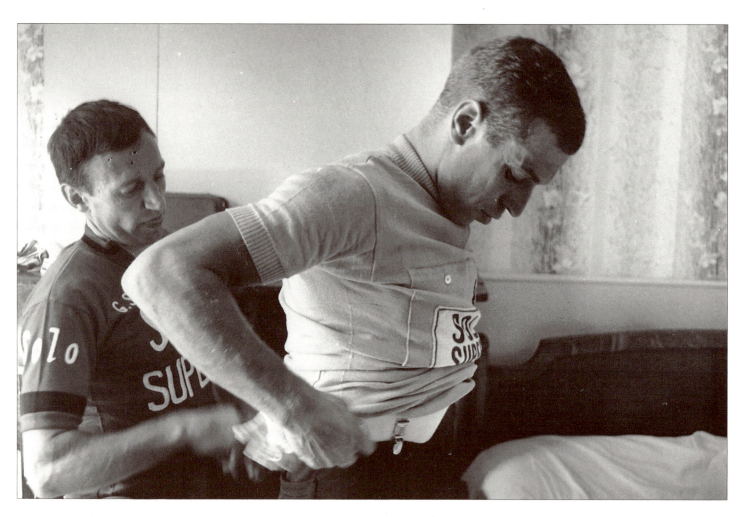

Edgar Sorgeloos had the rare priviledge to share a bedroom with his team leader.

able to dictate. Van Looy was his own boss and he laid down the rules and established the rituals. He would tolerate no tardiness and no outbursts. Each morning they awoke and around eight o'clock travelled the roads, which were forbidden to trucks, that went from Salo to Riva del Garda. They rode two-by-two, on a line, one kilometer each relay. At the end of the day training became intensified, taking on the form of real competition around Garde Lake, where the local populace watched them threading the highway, enhaling smoke from the passage of heavy trucks which sped alongside puffing their way towards Piacenza.

In the afternoon, Van Looy devoted his time to home training sessions in the hotel boiler room, wearing a thick pullover and skin tight jersey. He managed his career like an ascetic but could easily empty a case of beer, giving him an extra reason to toughen up his body with training. He was so meticulous that he had his tires custom

made in red, the color of his jersey and had his bicycle frames made to fit the demanding nature of the classics. In the Paris-Roubaix race he used a bicycle with a special front fork and reinforced his saddle for the pave sections, plus some seven-year-old tires. They were still so good that he had only one flat during fifteen races. "I always had to have one wrench on me or nearby because he just had to fool with his seat or his water bottle during the race," reported Edgar Sorgeloos. In any case, he did not want to be dependent on the technical support car.

His concern for perfection made him a tyrant. At Faema he decided everything: his teammates sleeping time, the bonus distribution, and the tactics for the upcoming race. "He abhorred repeating the same thing twice," Sorgeloos said. On the other side he left it up to Guillaume Driessens to maintain the necessary connivance against the other teams in order to attract sympathy in the classics' finale. Van Looy was

very suspicious and could be vindictive. Thus, he fired Julien Stevens after finding out that the latter was getting ready to leave him to join Eddy Merckx. "He forgot me in the bonus sharing," recalled Stevens, "and refused to talk to me after I had given him the best years of my career. At the end, he even arranged to have me excluded from the Criterium, where the racers of my generation earned their living." He was called "Emperor Rik" by even his most faithful critics, in view of his severe lack of emotional feelings. Raymond Impanis had a bitter experience when he had to forfeit at the very beginning of the Giro. "I finished second in the Romandie Tour after leading in most of the uphill climbs," he said. "I ran like God's fire but the flu kept me in bed and I had to give up the Giro. Rik never acknowledged the true reason. He felt that I was saving myself for the Tour. For that reason, I had to change teams."

From 1958 to 1962 Van Looy, with his

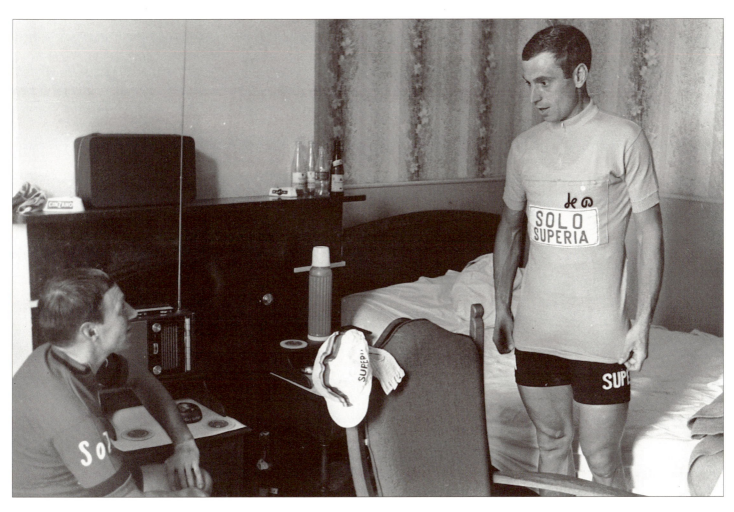

He helped his leader to wear the yellow jersey.

"Red Guard", built for himself a "palmares" that measured up to the personal goals that he had set, in a unique demonstration of performance. He gave himself to all the classics; winning Paris-Roubaix three times, also two Paris-Tours, and two World Championships (the second one coming in 1961). At Bern, his back wheel collapsed as soon as he crossed the finish line. He also made numerous incursions in the Tour de France, where he negotiated each stage of the race like he was directing the rhythm of a classic. He ran the race as though he were retiring the next day. His image was so strong and his presence so omnipotent that critics waited to see him "jump" Anquetil on his own turf. Run over by a motorcycle in 1962 at the bottom of the Pyrenees, sliced open by his own brakes during a fall in 1964 at Lisieux, he knew distress, but the green jersey which he earned for himself in 1963 gave him a clear increase in popularity.

Experts considered him the biggest clas-

sics "hunter" that the cycling world had yet encountered. He desecrated the Paris-Roubaix by getting rid of his theatrics and overcame Coppi in the hearts of numerous fans (Van Looy raced for an Italian team), but he soon had to admit that with the coming of Eddy Merckx, that 'power' could soon be changing hands. In 1965 the two men crossed each other at Solo Superia, where Van Steenbergen ended his career and Eddy Merckx quickly changed teams.

"Rik was extremely jealous of Eddy," Julien Stevens noticed, "and I remember his anger when Eddy won in San Remo. He couldn't handle the fact that we had let Eddy get ahead, even if in his heart he knew there was nothing he could do against the Brusselian." At first Merckx refused to answer back to Van Looy's provocations, which were aimed at ruining his life.

Their antagonism peaked in the Denderleuve Criterium where the two men distanced themselves from the group

accompanied by the cheering whistles of their fans. In 1968 Van Looy took the Fleche Wallone, the only classic missing from his "palmares". Then, the following year, Merckx put an end to thirty years of defeat for Belgium by winning the Tour de France. It was at that time, when a clear turnaround in public opinion occured. On August 10, 1970, at 36 years of age, the "Emperor of Herenthal" wound up in eighth place in the Kermesse de Walkenswaard race. So on a deserted road that brought him home he decided it was time to retire. His "Red Guards" had dispersed, his beautiful season in the sun had ended. "In the middle of the group, I felt like a stranger," he would admit a couple of years later.

He had refused to produce one last time on the trail of Anvers and it had been more than twenty years since he had patiently erased the tracks of former racing legends. He retired, refusing interviews and the accompanying worldliness they brought.

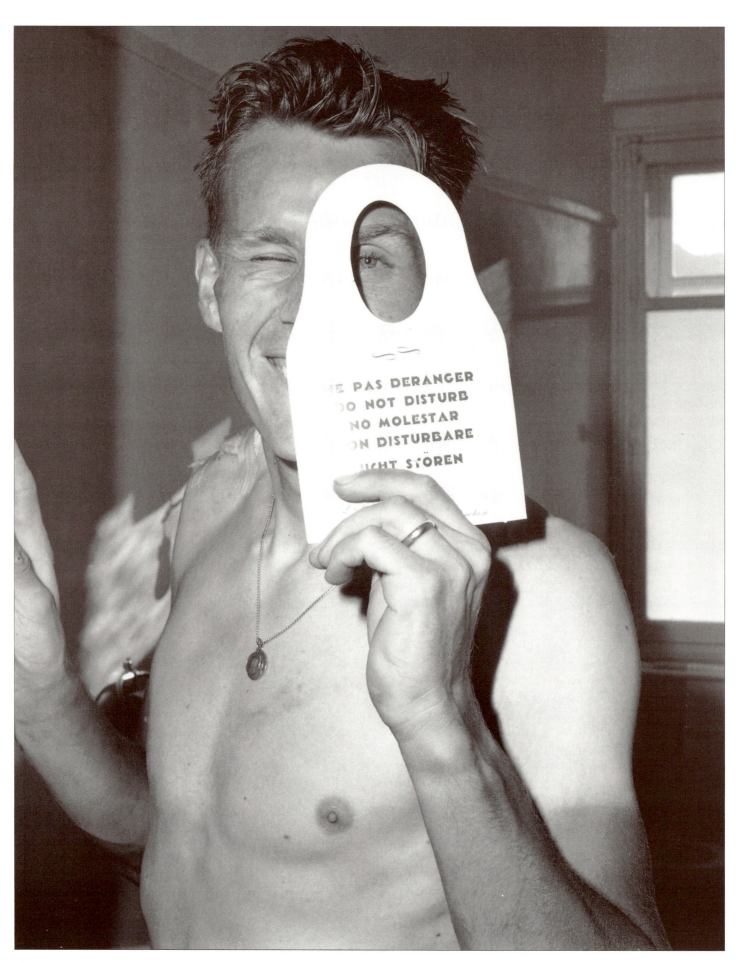

<figure>
The door hanger reads:

NE PAS DERANGER
DO NOT DISTURB
NO MOLESTAR
NON DISTURBARE
NICHT STÖREN
</figure>

JAN JANSSEN

Jan Janssen had two loves: the Tour de France, and his daughter, to whom he reserved his quiet moments of relaxation.

RAYMOND POULIDOR

The first pictures of him are dated from the 1962 Tour de France. They show him with his hat over the eyes, absentminded like he always was, exalted and pathetic at the same time, unlucky and discreet, with a cast on his left hand. In Jacques Anquetil, Poulidor had discovered a worthwhile adversary. Two years later, always with Anquetil, locked in their tragic "huit clos", eye-for-an-eye, tooth-for-a-tooth duel on the Puy-de-Dome hills, harangued by the crowds, often estimated at over 500,000 people. Then in 1968, with a bloody nose, after hitting a moped which had strayed onto the race course on Albi's road; and with Jean Pierre Genet, his most loyal teammate, who had offered him his spare tire; always in pain, a haggard look on his face, one foot over the precipice and saved by the strong, firm hand of Jacque Godet in the downhill portion of the Portet d'Aspet in 1973; Poulidor debonair or malicious posing patiently for posterity beside Antonin Magne and Marcel Bidot. Once again in the Tour de France because he loved the Tour more than anything else. Another time demonstrating the characteristics of a good Samaritan, then stalking Pingeon during the ascent of the Galiber; finally the photos show him disenchanted; always behind Eddy Merckx nearly 20 years after his debut but still close to Ralphael Geminiani and Louison Bobet.

When he turned professional in 1960 Poulidor became the heart of the Mercier team, after Bernard Gauthier recommended him to the director of that group. At that point in time, Jacques Anquetil monopo-lized the press, but his steady success began to bore the public. Reporters quickly seized upon the new star, a native of Creuse who was born to a family of share-croppers and who possessed a simplicity which stood out in sharp contrast to the "bourgeois" allure of the Norman (Anquetil). Their rivalry, which split them for more than ten years, displayed two men as dissimilar as could be. The gifted racer against the relentless climber. The defiant man and champion of failed opportunities versus the living incarnation of French capitalism. Within this context Poulidor became the subject of scrutiny and dissection for numerous sociologists, who analyzed and attempted to explain the phenomenom of "Poulidorism". As a social and cultural phenomenom, Poulidor serves as a reference. In the newspaper *Le Monde*, Pablo de la Huguera said in irony "the only good thing in France that works is Poulidor" and in the regard of Robert Escarpit, whose stock rose dramatically the day after the elections, "apparently if you have to make a choice, the next time I will vote for Poulidor. Poulidor is genuine. Even outside the world of cycling, he lives the life of a peaceful family man, worried about protecting his private life at St. Leonard de Noblat. We never saw him in town and we had to wait until his fall on Albi road to discover the face of his wife, Gisele, coming to show her concern and affection. Contrary to Anquetil, who dressed well and liked to display his expensive lifestyle, Poulidor was always dressed in a simple cotton sweat shirt. He put every penny he earned into real estate. One man lived a reasonable life while the other enjoyed transgressing the forbidden".

They evolved into two separate contexts far from each other. Jacques Anquetil lived in association with Raphael Geminiani, his old road partner, and Louison Bobet. He was a truculent person, audacious and open to new ideas, enjoying a stimulating lifestyle.

Poulidor linked his destiny with Antonin Magne. Pragmatic and conservative even when day after day he would feel humiliation at the hand of Anquetil. Tonin told Poulidor, "you have a name that will please the public. It is a golden name", but each time Tonin recruited a new racer to the Mercier team, he submitted the Limousin (Poulidor) to the test of his famous stopwatch. About Poulidor, Tonin made this statement, "Right away I knew this boy had exceptional physical qualities. I also discovered that the month of July will be unlucky or unfavorable to him and this revelation is upsetting to me. Will he be subjected to an implacable fatality? In France there will soon be only two parties: the Anquetilian side attracting the elite class and formed by those who prefer style to efficiency versus the Poulidorian party, more popular and attracting the more numerous poor."

For more than ten years these two men competed head to head on the sports field. Victory for one meant defeat for the other. Their battles symbolized the eternal struggle between rich and poor, country boy against city boy; the plebian versus the aristocrat; the frugal and the free spender. They divided opinions but their two cliques unified to make the Tour de France

"He wore his malediction like a virtual coat of shining armor." (Antoine Blondin)

a publicity instrument and thus ordained cycling as the number one sport in France.

Poulidor did not have any metaphysical problems. He accepted his defeats and he kept to himself, not to formulate critical opinion at the expense of his rival thinking maybe next time it could be him. He showed his warm human side to the cold side of the Norman and while he did not fight his popularity, he did not encourage it either, conscious of the advantages it could proffer his rival. Poulidor confided that "within the group, other racers never gave me gifts. Quite the contrary, the more my popularity rose, the more misery they heaped upon me." He made this remark towards the end of his career.

"Alley-vous Poupou!" (Go Poupou!) For more than fifteen years, that cheer unleashed the public like a rallying cry. One could see it on the banners carried by his fans, on a burning hot pavement written in white letters, on factory walls, or simply on a poster. "Poupou" was king! Some might consider "Poupou" to be a derisive term (would Anquetil like to be called Jacquot?... no) but the Limousan (Poulidor) welcomed it as a sign of affection from his cycling fans.

At first the superiority of the Norman (Anquetil) did not bother the Limousan (Poulidor) since it was so natural and evident and seemed to be written in his genes; and since Anquetil had won the Grand Prix de Nations in front of Koblet at the age of seventeen. Like many other cyclists, Poulidor suffered from a complex as he faced the one called "Master Jacques" on the account of his metronome regularity for winning and his capacity to influence the outcome of the races by his abundant knowledge about the personalities of his competitors. When facing Bahamontes, Rik Van Looy, Roger Riviere or Charley Gaul, the Norman knew exactly how to psyche out his rivals and convince them of their comparative inferiority,

and Poulidor fell into that trap. With the assistance of age, the distance diminished between the two combatants; their war had reached a point in 1964 where each man wanted to back out of the 1964 Tour de France, and this marked a decisive upturn in their antagonism towards one another.

That year Anquetil came back exhausted from competing in the Tour d'Italy and Poulidor ran a much better race against the clock. (The preceding year hadn't he won the Grand Prix de Nations ahead of the Belgian Ferdinand Bracke, the future world record holder?) For the first time Poulidor felt the Tour de France was in his hands, but he lost 20 seconds when Van Looy fell in front of him the first day. At Monaco he took a corner too soon and there was the Norman taking advantage of that mistake. He and Anquetil made equal gains in the race "against the watch" at Peyehorade-Bayonne, but then he fell 37 seconds behind as a result of a flat tire. Another problem occurred in the long race of Envalira when his mechanic failed to properly repair a broken spoke. During the big race at Puy-de-Dome Poulidor took the lead less than one kilometer from the summit, but that valiant effort proved too late to reclaim the yellow jersey, which remained on the shoulders of the Norman, due to a mistake of 14 little seconds. At the Parc, "Poupou" fell 54 seconds behind Anquetil, raising the question of why he didn't make an earlier start at Geant d'Auverne. While the question remained unanswered, students of cycling attribute it to Poulidor's inner belief in the invulnerability of Anquetil. In the Norman's absence there would always be one to dominate, the Italian racer Felice Gimondi in 1965, Lucien Aimar in 1966, Roger Pingeon in 1967 and later on, on the other side of his long career, there would be Eddy Merckx for sure, followed by Luis Ocana, Van Impe and Thevenet.

In 1968 conditions were ripe for Poulidor to finally win the Tour de France. Anquetil was in pre-retirement, Felice Gimondi was recuperating from exhaustion, and young Eddy Merckx was regarded as too young to even be starting in the "Grand Boucle" (the Great Circle"). In addition the Limousan could count on the unwavering support of a homogenous tricolor team devoted to his cause.

"For Raymond, it will be this year or never", announced Marcel Bidot, adding ... "but I sincerely believe that this is the year". All France hoped for victory for the Limousan, persecuted by the bad luck of the previous year. Then victim of a fall in the Platzerwassel, Poulidor had gone back on the road with a loaned bicycle (from Edward Delberghe) before collapsing in the Alsace Balloon, where he had covered his last kilometer at 15km per hour, a time slower than Pottier did in 1906. The same bad luck could not be repeated year after year...could it?

From Vittel to Bayonne via Luxembourg and Belgium the 1968 Tour began it's long preamble, and was judged as too fastidious by reporters. In Font-Romeu where the Tour actually started, rumor had it that a young Nordic, Jose Samyn was about to be kicked out of the race on account of drugs. Then there were reports of litigation by those who had opposed Felix Levitan at the college for reporters, but finally little was being said of the Limousan, who occupied a priviledged position as "5th rank General", preceded by Van den Berghe, Schiavon, Passuello and Pintens. "We had not hoped for so much," Marcel Bidot analyzed while rubbing his hands together, "Raymond has not yet stroked a pedal and has already made gains upon Van Springel, Brake and Janssen, who are his most dangerous rivals."

Then came the continuation of "the prophecy". On the morning of July 14, Marcel Bidot advised his tricolor team to

Poulidor faces his public on the track at the Park of Princes; after nearly twenty years of racing the Limousan was an indispensable personality in the History of the Tour.

exercise the most elementary prudence, knowing from experience that anything can happen in that long race of transition. To divert attention and possibly win the race, Roger Pingeon passed Poulidor during an offensive on the Coast of Chappelle, which is 100 kilometers from Albi. As winner of the Tour the previous year the Bugist (Pingeon) dug his lead out with determination coupled with his pedaling, which seemed derived from pure nervous energy. Pingeon was then 13 minutes ahead at that portion of the race, 60 kilometers from the finish line. Behind him however, some problems arose within the first group. From behind, Poulidor surprises Janssen, Brake, and Van Springel and passes them. It would seem the French had the situation well in hand, when the drama occurred. A moped skids out on to the course ahead of the cyclists. Bicycles shatter along with screams of terror. Poulidor is in this group. His nose bleeds terribly. Avoiding the crash, Aimar and Janssen sprint ahead, with speedometers oscillating between 55 and 60 kilometers per hour. Attended by four of his teammates, Jean Pierre Genet, Bernard Guyot, Anatole Novak and Christian Raymond, the Limousan went back on the road. Together the team was able to limit the "damage", conceding one hour and five minutes to their rivals. While on his descent, Poulidor forgetting his wounds burst out with "we don't attack when a man is on the ground", speaking of Janssen, "Jacques himself would never do that". This small comment was not lost on the reporters. While he did not say Anquetil specifically, they all knew who "Jacques" was and this affectionate tone led to what became a closeness between the two old rivals.

It is still July 14, 1968 and Poulidor's foreboding of the loss of the Tour, which was supposed to be his, seems to be coming true. So drawing upon inner strength and courage Poulidor takes the lead in the Aurille part of the race and crossed into the celebrated Coast of Montsaly, which had proved fatal to Bobet, without any problem. However, at this point his heart just wasn't there. He had great difficulty breathing and did not know how to rid himself of a migraine headache. On the

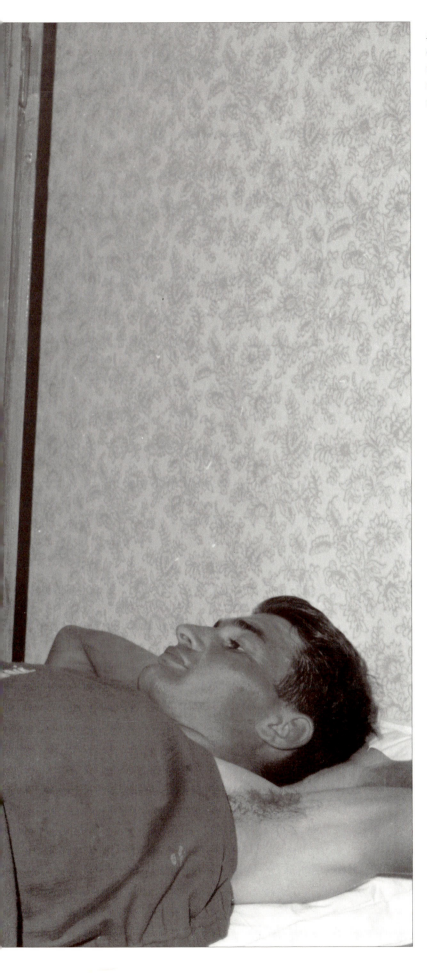

In the hands of the old Leoni, with whom he reviewed the race course.

previous evening, X-rays revealed a fractured nose plus slight cranial trauma. Following a sleepless night, he took the advice of his doctor, who advised him he should give up the race. On July 16 Poulidor stayed in his room at the appropriately named Hotel Terminus, next to the train station in Aurillac. His wife, Gisele, came to join him. Facing the many reporters who paraded by his bedside, Poulidor remained dignified. He was nevertheless disfigured and the same could be said for the Tour.

"What do you think...this had to happen to me, right!" he blurted out. "It is the risk of the profession and I don't want to complain. I came out pretty good, so let's not talk about bad luck, but if you talk about bad luck, look at Riviere who cannot now even ride his bicycle. For myself I will always have the possiblity to win it next year."

On the Vincennes municipal road, when Jan Janssen tore the yellow jersey off the Belgian Van Springel, Marcel Bidot said farewell to the Tour de France, which he had discovered some 42 years earlier. The old man could not help but cry like he had cried as a child and also as he had cried the previous year after Poulidor's fall at the bottom of the hill at Platzerwassel. This time, however, his sadness was accompanied by a certain bitterness, which he went on to explain: "If Antonin Magne had not opposed my vote, I would have taken Poulidor on the French National Team in 1961. This selection would have changed the face of cycling. Raymond Poulidor, who admired Anquetil could have formed a friendship with him not unlike that of Geminiani and Louison Bobet. They would have cooperated with each other instead of tearing each other apart. They would have dominated the world of cycling for at least ten years, and Poulidor would have won the Tour."

With the arrival of Eddy Merckx, the Limousan knew two years of floatation. Anquetil's retirement deprived him of his reparations. He had to face off with the Belgian in the classics, and to face the coming of the new generation, led by Bernard Thevenet, Cyrille Guimard, and Jean-Pierre Danguillaume. Antonin Magne wasn't there to advise him but his collabo-

He welcomed each event in his life with a fantastic resignation, it is without doubt why the French recognized themselves in him.

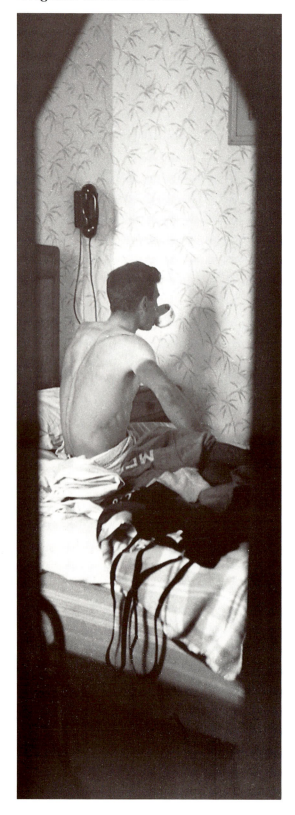

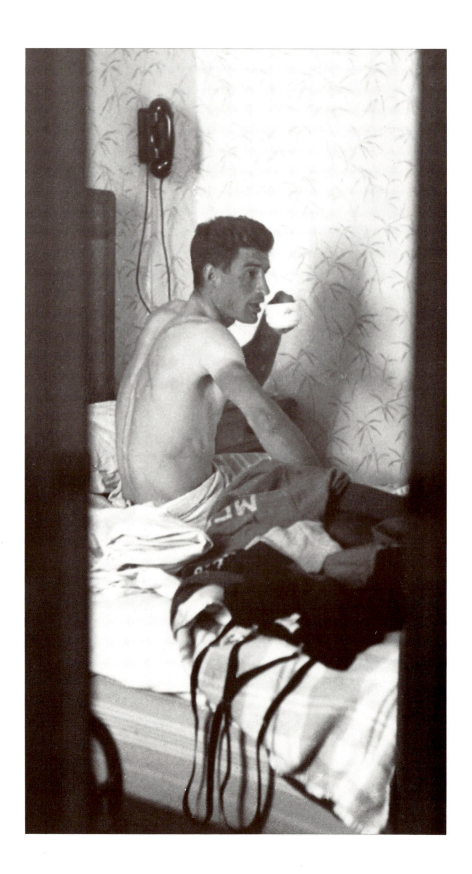

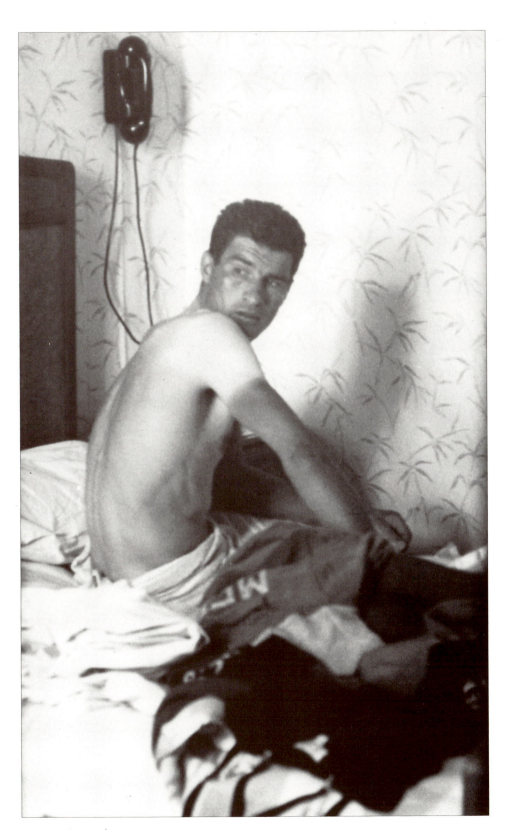

rations with Louis Caput proved to be profitable. In 1972, in his resurrection, to the general surprise of everyone, he takes the lead from Eddy Merckx in the chronometered uphill ascension of the Col d'Eze. At the conclusion at Paris-Nice there is stupor. Poulidorism refound its clamor of yesteryear, but this time, it was his longeveity that is acclaimed. This unbelievable longevity by itself erased all his past defeats. He came in second on the Fleche Wallone, beaten by Merckx again, second in the 1974 Tour, always second in the World Championship of Montreal (as expected, beaten by Merckx). Those who did not appreciate him at the time he opposed Anquetil, took to regret that this virtuous champion had never achieved the wearing of the Tour's yellow jersey, even for one day. In 1967, he was defeated by six seconds in the prologue behind the Basque Jose-Maria Errandenoea.

It will never be known which should be credited with Poulidor's wins. Should the credit go to Poulidor himself, or his bad luck, which had made him stronger. His resurrection created a new kind of hero, to the point where the personality of a true champion showed through. At the end of the '60s he only needed to show up and he made the event with his humor and personality. When Poulidor fell, it was the Tour that went down.

He was the most popular French champion of this time, and interested parties could never fully explain this strange phenomenon. There was no doubt that the man in the street saw himself in Poulidor, because of life's maltreatment and as one who had accepted bad luck with a good sense of humor.

He would one day say, "My big luck was to have lots of bad luck."

He could have said that his luck had a name, Jacques Anquetil. When Anquetil retired on December 25, 1965, at the Wambrechies cyclo-cross, Poulidor ex-

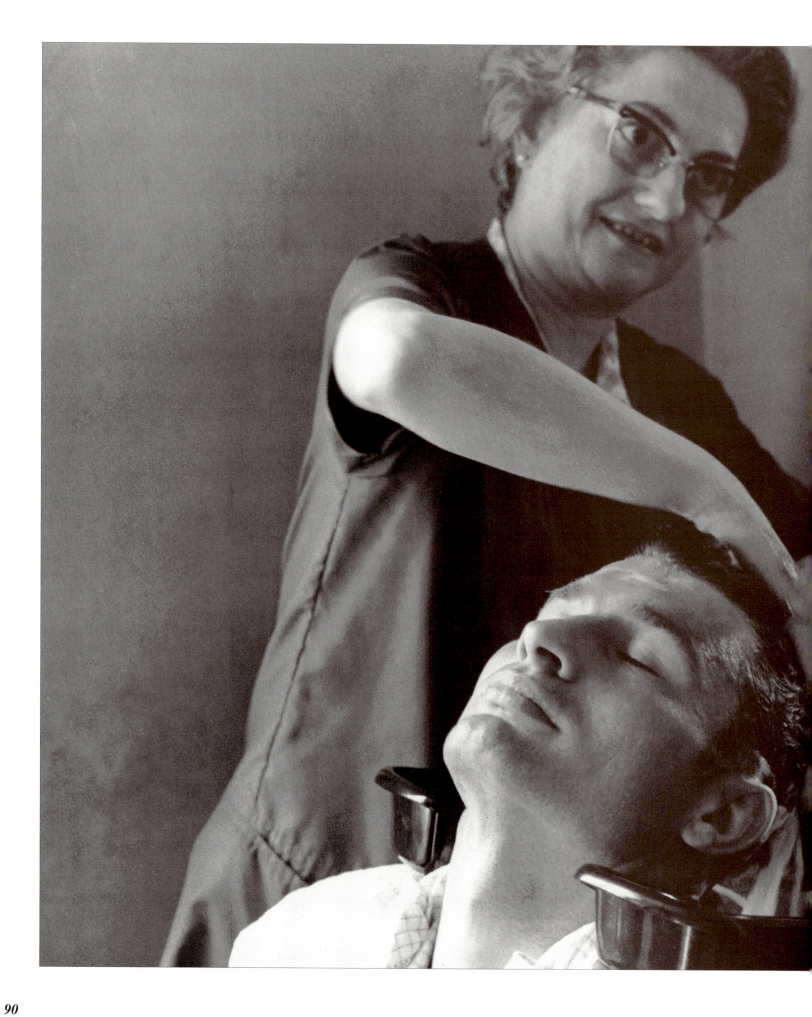

pressed no regret. After escaping from the Anquetillian era, he survived Merckxism with grand style, his advanced age placing him well ahead of the rivals similar to the Belgian, who maintained friendships with Luis Ocana, Jose Manuel Fuente, Joop Zoetemelk and Felice Gimondi. What could he regret? He worked himself to death up to the celebrity ceiling without ever having had to win the Tour de France. He never placed blame for his losses on his bad luck which overwhelmed him on more than one occasion. Maybe if it wasn't for a fourth flat tire in the 1975 finale of the Paris-Roubaix, he would not have been outdistanced by the lead group on his 40th birthday.

He might attribute his defeats in the Tour to his bad genie. Most of the time, he was content to follow, leaving the others to take the initiative, and so it was then that Gimondi came to pass him on the way to Rouen, that Lucien Aimar surprised him on the downhill run of the mountain pass of Coletta, and that Pingeon left him behind on the way to Jambes. Poulidor rarely weighed the events. He had faults in his makeup. He lacked the rage within him to win and which destiny makes possible.

At times, he could not be excused from blame. He did not always give sufficient attention to the quality of his entourage, and his teammates were not always rewarded in proportion to the services they rendered. Poulidor was frugal in all senses of the term: he was frugal with words, encouragement, thankfullness and with money. Like many of those who come from nothing, he was afraid to end with

nothing. This fault completed his isolation from the rest of his peers, because in this group, friendship was based on money. It is give and give, and the one who spends the most receives the most rewards. It is a known fact that in order to maintain allies, to assure, if necessary the support of his rival in the last kilometer of a classic, that one must be owed a favor before he can collect it. Poulidor gave out little and he received back very little. In that area, Poulidor was not known as a team player. In 1966, it was thanks to the complicity of Franco Bitossi and of Rudi Altig that Lucian Aimar had won the Tour on the way to Turino. Months before, Jacques Anquetil didn't hesitate to bribe a big portion of the group to strip that same Poulidor of the leader's white jersey in the last stage of the Paris-Nice race. The latter would cry scandal, but he was beaten in the rules, the non-written rules, but rules that had been solidly established.

On the contrary, the qualitative "eternal second" description which stuck to his skin was just a myth, a superficial chronicle of an easy way of talking. Poulidor was better than that. In his 15-year career, he had won the French Championship, Milan-San Remo (after wanting to give up on the coast of Varazze), the Fleche-Wallone, the Tour d'Espagne, the Grand Prix des Nations... without counting the multitudes of various stages of the most significant portions of the grand Tours...

He had made a beautiful palmares, (list of wins), but other than himself, who cared?

All had passed, as though Anquetil was condemned to wear the yellow jersey and Poulidor to suffer against the polka dot.

FEDERICO BAHAMONTES

*King of the mountains after six stages of the race,
Bahamontes was a fantastic person, and very moody;
few people could reason with him when he suddenly
decided to abandon. His entourage evoked the grandeur
of Spain, but God the Father nor all the saints could
make him change his mind.*

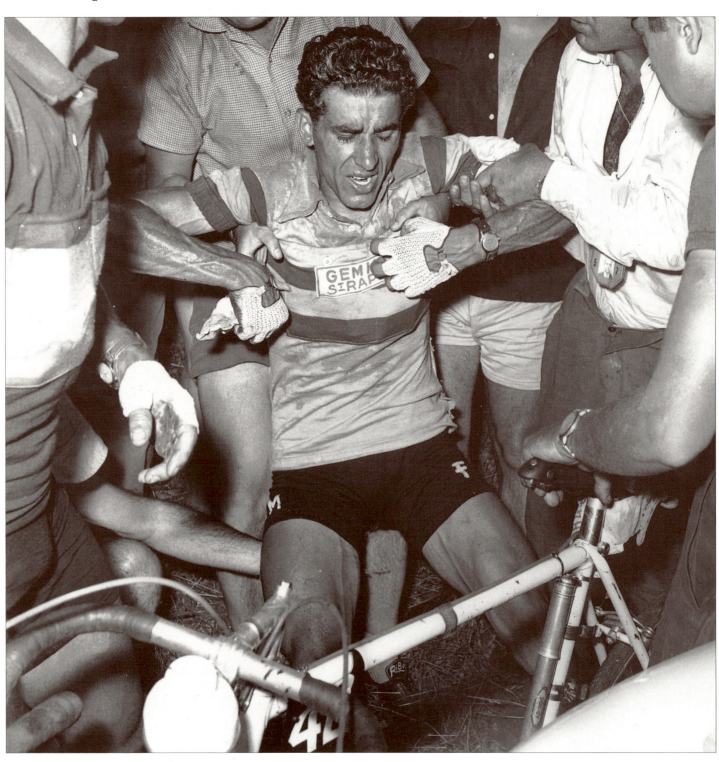

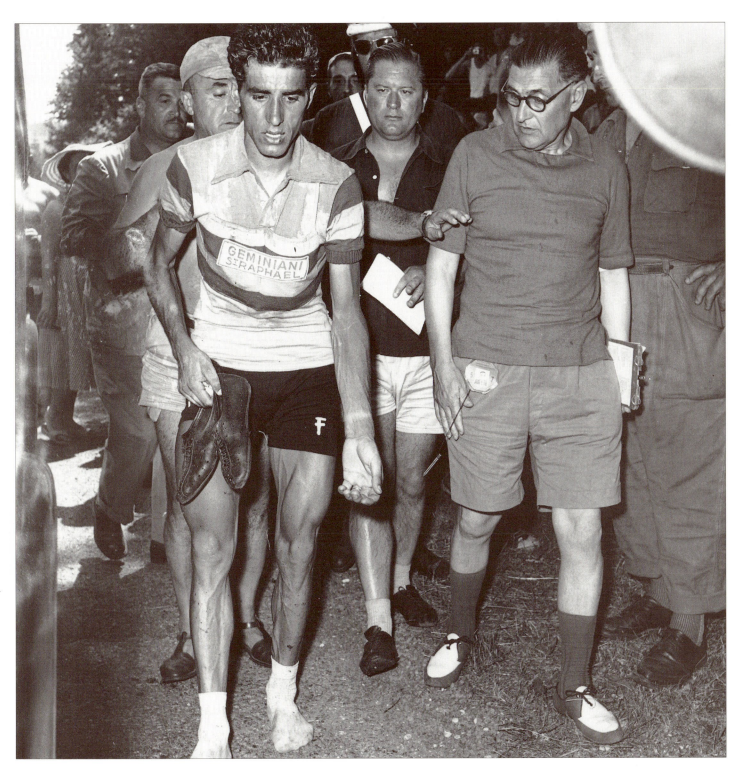

In 1957, discouraged to find himself alone after the retreat of Miguel Poblet, he quit the race on tiptoe after removing his shoes as a final sign of his determination.

With his small step like Chaplin, Babamontes had returned to the Dunkerque station where he would take the first train in the direction of Spain. His luggage in one hand, his bicycle in the other, he expressed the ingratitude of his life as an artist.

He was beautiful like a Donatello.

GIANNI MOTTA

When the cycling world unleashed Rik Van Looy and Tom Simpson on the pink pavement of Intelvi, he went alone in the Lombardie Tour and Italy thought it had found it's new messiah. He would be Fausto Coppi's and Gino Bartali's proud successor, the modern apostle of offensive cycling. His name was Gianni Motta. He was only a beginner in the professional season, but he had everything going for him, with a handsome face similar to the looks of Victor Emmanuel of Savoy. He had faintly pink skin and legs so muscular that it appeared they were sculpted by Michelangelo himself.

Under the blue and tan jersey, his healthy looks contrasted with his country of Italy, which was in such bad shape. There were, to be sure, good racers beyond the Alps; Ercole Baldini, haloed by his time record; Nino de Filippis, capable of both the best and the worst, and let us not forget Pambianco, Balmanion, or Taccone who was a Tuscan full of haughtiness, but they were only pale comparisons to the legendary past Italian champions like Binda, Girardengo, Coppi and Bartali. None of the aforementioned secondary racers compared to this new twenty-one year-old stallion, under his royal allure was concealed a youngster with a burning desire to win. He was first noticed at Gropello, one of those sad market towns which were strung out along the Bergame

coast where the smog was dense and everywhere one could smell the stench of gas, asphalt, burned rubber and see the smoke pouring from the trucks that clogged the roads from Val d'Aoste to Trentin.

Motta tried to forget his miserable childhood, a childhood that followed him like some long spell of insomnia, even though he now had fame and glory. He saw his father and brothers working so hard on that stingy land, condemned to the life of farmers. At the Motta home bread was bitter and the existence so harsh that it molded the body as it strengthened the heart. The whole family slept close to one another and ate polenta while chickens scratched in the dirt. The first thing each morning they would look out the window at their land to be sure it was still there and the way they had left it. "At the top of his career, Gianni was afraid to sleep in his champion's clothes for fear he would wake up in the skin of a support rider," said former reporter Maria Fossati. Swampy and cold, Lombardy had forced him to become the way he was; worried and tormented, in search of acknowledgement, because for Motta, poverty was more than a state of mind...more than a social condition.

In less than one year in the professionals, he became a legend, because he backed up all his impudence with equal talent. Fifth in his first Giro in 1964, he

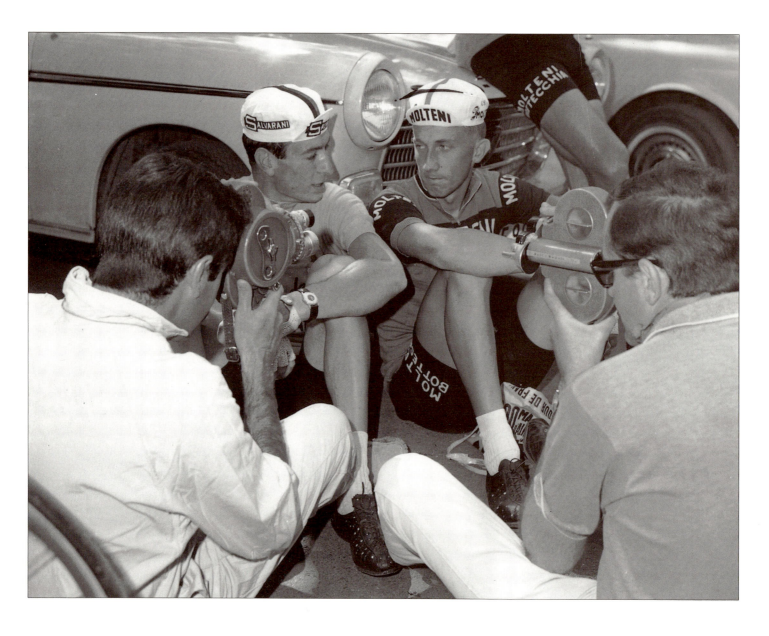

came in behind Anquetil, Zilioli, De Rosso and Ardoni. He also shone in the Six Jours, where the "Kings of the Road" and the "Godfathers of Cycling" always won. Peter Post and Rik Van Steenbergen treated him with the respect that was usually reserved for cycling's "prima donnas". (He would win the Six Jours, presumed a shoo-in for the Belgian.) His career was launched, but if he was immediately a notorious champion, he would also be the declining champion for a very long time.

In 1965, he seemed destined for glory, when he was run over by a car in the Mosses mountain pass on the summit of the Romandie Tour. He tore his miniscus and had to back out of the Giro's race. Two months later, barely back on his feet he took the lead in the Tour de France,

greeted by people who thought him superior to Raymond Poulidor, then the favorite to win in the absence of Anquetil. However, one thing no one had counted on was Poulidor being beaten by Felice Gimondi, a twenty-one year-old Bergasque, who was unknown to the public. It was a huge surprise. Third in that trial, Motta lost no respect but public opinion turned in favor of his Italian rival, Gimondi. Motta conceded with bitterness and was totally disappointed by the attitude of Raymond Poulidor. "In the descent of Vars' Mountain I tried to incite Poulidor to race with me, but to my surprise, the Frenchman refused. I don't understand why," Gianni implored. "We only needed to reach the bottom of the Izoard together to shake everything up and then one of us

would win the Tour!"

After his return to Italy, Gianni had a strange feeling that things had gotten away from him. Less than one year after being exalted as the "new" Coppi and with manners like Carlesi, Zilioli and many others, he found himself like Bartali, forced to put up with the hassles that Gimondi gave him. Their "duel" governed the life of the transalpin cycling world, proving profitable to the press, which enjoyed amplifying their royal antagonism. It reached its paroxysm in the springtime of 1966, which had been very favorable for Gimondi. In the middle of the Romagne race Gimondi heard that his rival (Motta) had won the Paris-Brussels Tour, and he was more than furious. At the finish line he was overwhelmed with rage at Dino Zandegu,

Under the eyes of the camera,
Gimondi and Motta. Their
rivalry would split Italy.

whom he knew to be faster than himself. "But what has gotten into Motta!" exclaimed Zandegu, ignoring Gimondi's success in the Franco-Belgium race. "I've never seen him like that. In the last kilometers nobody could relay him. He was as furious as a cat caught by the tail under a subway!"

Hurt by the critics, who were siding with Gimondi, the Lombardian made himself known in the Giro, with the blessings of Jacques Anquetil. The latter was happy to impede the Bergamasque in the triumphant march. Weeks later, showing his gratitude, Motta invited the Norman to race in the Gropello Criterium, where the Italian paid the champion's contract out of his own pocket. "Jacques didn't know it but I was happy to see him race in that poor little country of Gropello, knowing how popular he was in Italy, and I owed him more than a little," he said. The pink jersey was launched again. Everywhere people applauded by screaming Coppi's name.

Ernesto Colnago, who supported Gianni from the beginning encouraged him to make an attempt at the speed record. The designer had prepared an ultra-light bicycle and contacted the Vigorelli's director to insure everything would be in order but the Lombardian at first hesitated, then backed out because it was his dream to wear the rainbow jersey, hoping to swing the pendulum of public opinion back in his direction, and that dream became an obsession.

To succeed in that goal, Motta put himself under the wing of Dr. De Donato. The doctor was a strange person, who had worked for three years in a Soviet Union Biochemistry Laboratory. Dr. De Donato applied conditional psychological methods on his protege, such as those the cosmonauts had undergone. Henceforth, Motta trained at night, on distances approaching 100 kilometeres. He was on prolonged diets, fed on predigested food. He gulped down numbered wild herb drinks which was not surprising since the farmers in the

north of Italy believed in the benefits of plants and made drinks from wild herbs at home that were sold by street charlatans. He embarked on a quest for spiritual perfection but the search ended on the opposite side of the street, so to speak.

Motta believed strongly in his "Guru", who announced to reporters that his "foal" would make a joke out of his rivals (Merckx, Altig, Janssen and Gimondi) on the Heerlen Circuit. Motta forgot his lengendary prudence. He declared his intention to attack at the very beginning of the race: "I feel capable of making three hundred kilometers in the lead by myself," he claimed.

A psychodrama broke out in the middle of the squadron, because the Lombardian refused to eat at the common table. "There's nothing to understand," Ardoni commented, "his doctor has him brainwashed." Blinded by the influence of the doctor, Motta looked happy. He feared neither distance nor defeat, not even Gimondi worried him. He did not even complain about his left leg, which chronically ached.

On the day of the race he kept his promise and carried out a violent attack on the seventh kilometer, in the company of Merckx, Van der Vleuten and the Spaniard Ramon Saez, who was the least known of the four. Jan Janssen joined them later, and the events took an extremely disadvantageous downturn for Motta on the Heerlen pavement. Merckx won the sprint in front of Jan Janssen and Ramon Saez. Gianni Motta found his defeat very hard to swallow indeed.

"I am convinced that I would have won this championship if Janssen had not joined us," Gianni said, "because after that, Merckx and Saez did not want to race. They were afraid to be beaten in the sprint. After all the promises I made, I couldn't get away but I am holding the Italian Team responsible for letting a man like Janssen go." The Lombardian became a victim of his own ingenuity, robbed of his title, which he thought he very well deserved,

and defeated by the critics, who reproached him for Gimondi's loss.

"He abused our trust," declared some members of the squadron, now happy to put him in his place. To each his story. Gianni Motta was an authentic champion, full of good qualities but he had one flaw, and that was he allowed himself to come under the control of the doctor. After this defeat, he believed he was more persecuted than ever by the press, who said he was no longer able to confuse his opponents on the road.

A malignant and persistent pain made him slow down his activities. On certain days the pain was so great that he cried on his bicycle, in the shadows of the group. However, his physical pain was nothing compared to his emotional pain.

The last years of his career were chaotic. He had to beat the scepticism of the press, who knew that the Lombardian had committed grave errors in his preparation. He also had to fight against hostility from the "Gimondists", which had become greater. Motta passed most of his time in the psychiatrists offices, without any noticeable results. "By the way, from what was he suffering?" everyone asked. "Most people did not believe me, they thought I was dreaming. Some psychiatrists were happy to count me among their patients," Gianni said.

Then one day, Professor Cevese from Padoue University detected the origin of his pain, after watching Motta train for hours and following behind him at the wheel of his car. It was in August of 1970 after his best years had gone by in a haze, that the Italian was operated on for stenosis.

Barely recuperated, he beat Merckx on the Varesines Valley circuit and won six other races right by the numbers. In 1974, he left cycling after winning the first stage of the Giro at Milan. He left behind him the image of an incomplete champion, who with a little luck would have been among the biggest names in cycling history.

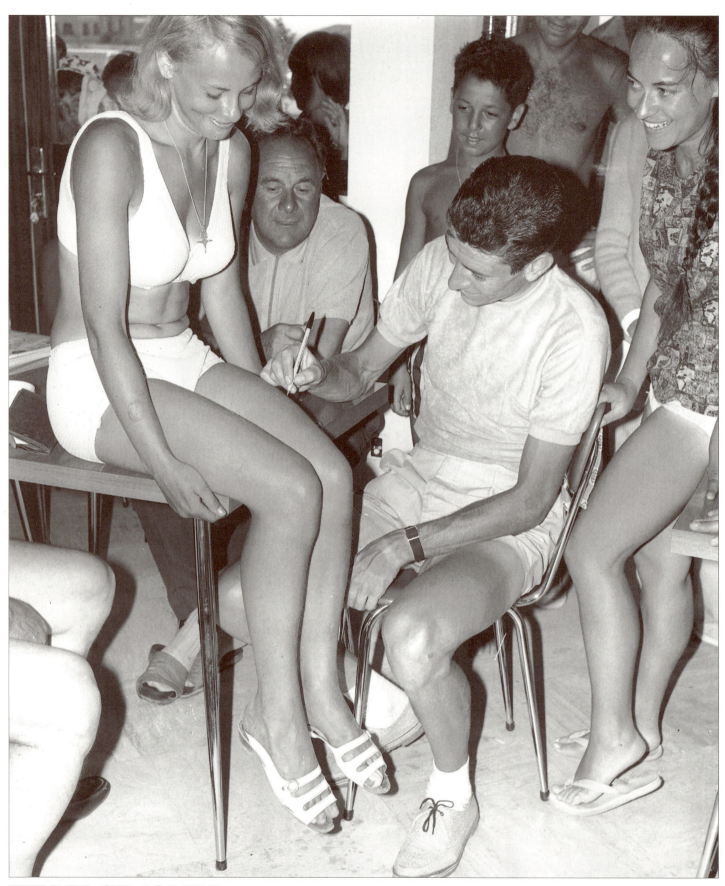

FELICE GIMONDI

In 1965, a new racer is seen in the arena left open by Anquetil. At 22 years of age, Felice Gimondi imposed himself as the leader of the new generation. The Italian had ambition and a pretty wife, whose picture he carried inside the cover of his suitcase. Even for her, he could not give up his faithfulness to his public...

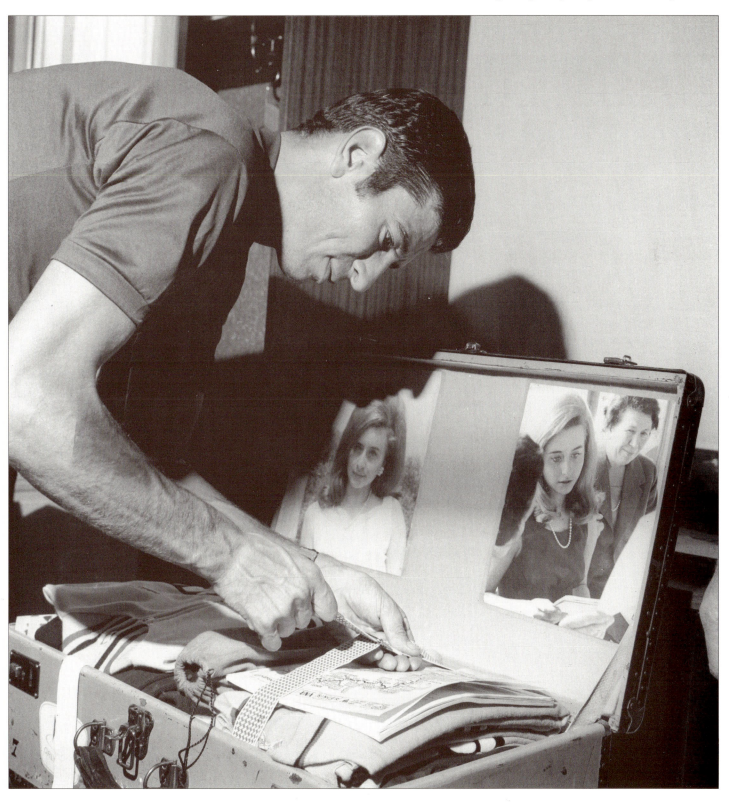

*He was the Hamlet
of cycling, tormented
by his inner conflicts.*

ITALO ZILIOLI

He was considered to be the best hope of his generation. He worked part time for Vincenzo Giacotta, manager for Carpano, until on the other end of the telephone a frail and broken voice got him out of his daydreams. He would have recognized that voice among any others, hearing it as on the RAI's microphone. It was the voice of Italy, Coppi's voice. His heart accelerated. "Quick, quick! It's me, Fausto." His emotions put a knot in his throat. "Can you hear me? It's me, Fausto. Pass me to Vincenzo."

He couldn't answer. He was only able to mumble some inaudible words. It was the only contact he ever had with Coppi, but this communication was the biggest event in his life. After that , he wove the conspiracy of his own legend, that of a super-sensitive and romantic person with a lonely childhood from which he could never repair the trauma.

Born in wartime and into an impoverished family, Italio Zilioli was so skinny and so puny that cycling technicians of the Transalpin were perplexed. How can so frail a body and emaciated face be so powerful on the road? By what alchemy? In 1963, he had subjugated his observers by winning four big national classics. In the uphill of Bochetta, the highest point of the Appenin's Tour, he exploded from the group, hands flat on the handlebars, straight torso, legs turning like a connecting rod in perfect synchronism.

With a troubled physiognomy, the Turinese offered a rare analogy with Fausto Coppi, the missing champion from whom he borrowed the emaciated face, the painful look, the style allied with power and gracefulness. From then on, experts saw in him not only the resemblence with the champion, but his reincarnation. They started calling him "Coppino" (the little Coppi), forcing him to answer to the long lines of fans, deceived by the repeated failures of their jurisdiction in the Tour de France where Coppi, Magni and Bartali had not been replaced. Zilioli lost his self assurance. Second in the 1964 Giro, behind Anquetil; second again in 1966, passed by Motta, whom Italy secretly wished would win the event. The following year, an incident happened in the Magella: when he found himself alone, well ahead of the group, with victory looking established, Zilioli is rejoined, then passed by a fireball, a balanced athlete looking like a sprinter.

It was Merckx's beginning years, the ending years for Motta, Gimondi, Ardoni and the likes; and in Zilioli the birth of a dull resignation, not mad enough to be in the lead ranks, maybe he felt it was his place. A dedicated Catholic, he looked at life with an angelic look, doing his job with a mixture of denial and suffering, without finding his balance in that narrow sharing.

"He never sleeps," Ardoni recalled. "At night he turns around, cries his fears and his disgust and ends by waking the other person who shares his bedroom. He needed to tell of his anxieties to feel better." Marino himself, remembered the one tragic night in the Abruzzes, at the house of Tirreno Adriatico: "He had wakened me, and I found him on top of the dresser. Italo had taken the team leader jersey and it had bothered him. He was sweating and had had a nightmare. In the morning he told me, 'Marino, I didn't close my eyes, I am dead, I am going to lose everything, even my cycling shirt!'"

In the stage races he loved to glide in the fresh shadow of a church to revive his faith. He put his suffering in God's hands. "I especially thanked him for giving me the strength to prolong, on the bicycle, my childhood dreams," he said. When his fame had declined with the public, he found an immense good luck and for him it was a blessing when he was recruited by Eddy Merckx into the heart of the Faemino Group. The "Cannibal" (Merckx) had in him, Zilioli, a devoted teammate and a good climber who did not ask for anything in particular except to be given respect and affection.

In the shadow of the Belgian champion, Zilioli refound the enthusiasm of his youth and took the yellow jersey in the 1970 Tour de France. He kept it for only four days, which justified, by themselves, all his past torments. It was with some luster that he managed dual combat against his opponents Gimondi, Anquetil and Motta, and his own convictions. He did not win either battle because he lacked some character, but he was in order with himself when he retired in 1976, at peace in strict anonymity.

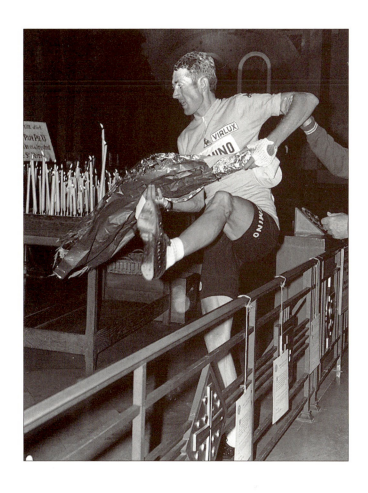

In the salon, Aimar takes his place as Poulidor attends his "Tour".

ROGER PINGEON

Jacques Anquetil had lived out the end of his reign, and the giant shadow of Eddy Merckx was profiled in all his lack of moderation when he won the 1967 Tour de France, after a charge on the road at Jambes. In the course of this transitional era, Roger Pingeon was sometimes sublime, indeed he was magnificent on certain days, but he had multiple reversals, and his frequent desertions gave him the image of an inconsistent, hypochondriacal, and taciturn champion. Some days he felt unlucky and claimed to suffer from fragile health. Typical for a stage racer, gifted in the climb, he lived his career in a permanent state of anxiety, waiting for a catastrophy. His most insignificant pain became the only object of his preoccupation. He was a man apart, monomanic and lonely, subject to some passing emotional crisis which would incite him, or on some depressing evenings, asking himself if perhaps it would be better to keep his job as a plumber. Barely a year after turning professional, he left the Paris-Nice race during a stage in Corse swearing he had had enough and it was the end.

"Today," he declared, "I not only give up Paris-Nice, but the cycling competition as well."

In 1968, a different incident: he arrived at the departure point for the Giro, but renounced racing at the last moment, without any valid excuse. Each time he decided to give it up, then would come back on that decision and the press was amused by his indecision. He was prey to violent mood swings. The most spectacular was in the 1969 Tour de France, when he slapped his teammate Raymond Delisle to punish him for exercising his personal agenda and not that of the team's.

Being discreet by nature, his desertions didn't have the truculence which surrounded Robic or Geminiani. He withdrew on tiptoe, after changing his wool jersey for a suit, and left for his new life somewhere waiting for him. He developed with pleasure a persecuted feeling, which on some days was his justification. Two examples of this, among others: In 1965, when he was getting ready to win the Midi-Libre, organizers made it known they would like a very prestigious laureat and a coalition was formed. The group protected the escape of Tom Simpson, victim of a flat tire, and it was Andre Fourcher, "Father Fouche", who won it. In the 1974 Tour de France, he slipped away in the company of the Belgian Ronald de Witte, but near Dieppe he went flat. To numerous racers, it was only a common incident, but not to Pingeon, who, crazy with rage, threw his bicycle into the air then stepped furiously on it when it landed. It was his last outburst, the end of a long frustration.

With a little luck, he could have won two other Tours de France; in 1968, if Marcel Bidot had shown trust in him; and in 1969, if Eddy Merckx, suspended for drugs since the Tour d'Italy (under strange curcumstances it is true), hadn't benefited from a measure of clemency from the FICP. Suspended for the same motive in 1971, Pingeon did not receive any favors and it encouraged him to perservere in the idea that justice was not on his side.

Author of a real exploit in 1967 on the road at Jambes, he was able to succeed by imposing his style, similar to that of Coppi. At that time, he was still young, but already unscrupulous. He refused to meet at the hotel of the bicycle racers, finding it unnec-

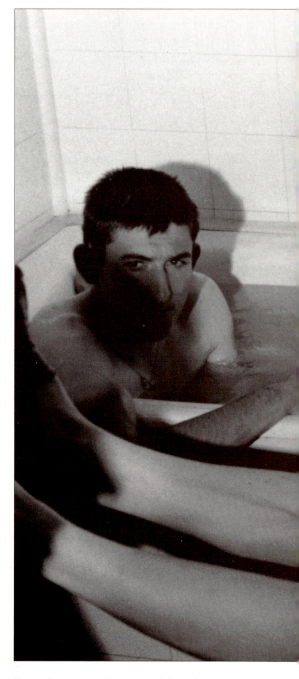

In order to not interrupt his relaxation, Roger Pigeon would give his interviews from his bath, where he would converse along with two other French teammates, Bernard Guyot (at left) and Christian Raymond.

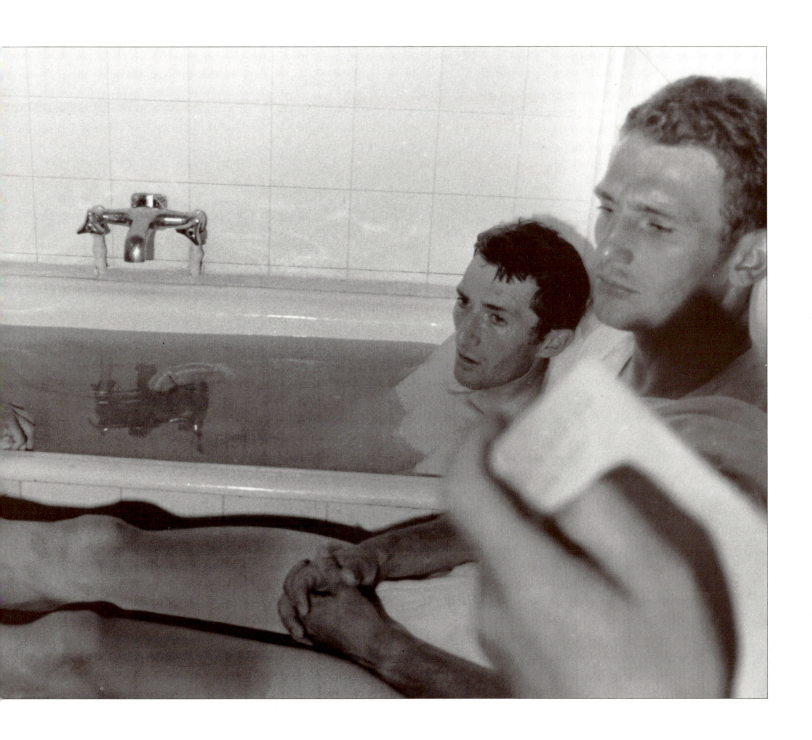

essary to add more fatigue to the day. His bedroom number was kept secret to avoid the groupies, and while he would never decline an interview, he would give it from his bathtub, because each minute counted. Pingeon considered time to the minute detail of a contract killer. He insisted on being the first to the massage table, and the last to the dinner table so that he did not have to succumb to the slow service. At a time when his teammates loved to enjoy each other's company and conversation, lucky to lift the stress from the day, he preferred to keep to himself.

"I didn't have a job like the others," he said, "so I didn't want to live like the others." He took care to study each day's race avidly and had a Michelin map collection that was coveted by others. And he would religiously consult the weather station. Before going to sleep he obstructed all the light in his bedroom, to the point where he stuffed the keyholes with cotton balls and slept with a bandana over his eyes. His trainer knew not to wake him until the last moment, half an hour after his teammates. He had calculated that in the duration of the Tour, this tactic gave him an extra night's sleep!

When his sun shined, when he didn't suffer from allergies, or an arthritic crisis hadn't paralyzed him...he was a most charming man.

*This dictator was an angel,
this sphinx was one to be
ecumenical and taciturn.*

EDDY MERCKX

Just the evocation of his name and memories come flooding back showing us the man he was, magnificent and secretive, in the ambivalent manner that was his character. We see him radiant with happinenss on the sidewalk in Herleen where he became World Champion in 1967; on the edge of a nervous breakdown, on his bed in shorts, tank top and suspenders after the completion of a Giro stage; both barbarian and winner on the northern pavements; with Baudouin and Fabiola, to the Palace steps after his first Tour in 1969; grazing the edge of the Blois Velodrome, where a miniscule mistake could mean his death; mussing the hair of Tom Simpson; on the overheated mountainside roads of Ventoux -- again Merckx both sublime and pathetic, expiating his faults and his distress in the Alps-Huez uphill climb, as though he always wanted to orchestrate his own agony; Merckx...always noble and so generous, besieged by the partisan crowd with their blind passion; Merckx...the man who was never afraid to express himself.

When he announced his retirement on May 18, 1978, Belgium, in tears, took to the veil for this incomparable champion. He entered into legend like we enter a convent. Merckx had escaped again, but this time for good and no one would ever catch him or equal him. His time had come and he crossed over into retirement without looking back, making our passion a dated tidal wave. Merckx preached austerity, when everyone else called for loose morals. He defended trampled values popular in the "flower years" of the sixties. He

was not a material being. We never saw him support a quarrel or take sides in the linguistic war which was splitting his country (Belgium). Sequestered in his job, cultivating his mystery without wanting it, fifteen long years dedicated to being at the top of his art, during which his relations with glory never surpassed the threshold which made Thevenet, Poulidor or Guimard surprisingly inaccessible.

By winning the 1969 Tour de France thirty years after Sylvere Maes, he appeased his country's neurosis, outraged by a dearth of victories that had lasted far too long. A thousand articles were dedicated to him. His win coincided with the birth of the first direct televised reporting and cameras never eluded his personna nor his dark secrets. Merckx sealed that alliance with his athletic grace and lack of moderation, and those who were of age to appreciate the span of his reign, his gestures, his splendor, they would be the ones who would preserve the memory of a very complex champion. He was paradoxical and at the same time dominating and vulnerable. Annihilated by the controversies of life, he was very disconcerted by the brutal disappearance of his manager, Jean Van Buggenhout. On the outside he appeared calm but inside he hid a tormented and worried soul. In the middle of the night before a big classic, he would awaken to heighten his bicycle seat a millimeter or correct the inclination of his handle bars before returning to bed totally appeased. This dictator was an angel. This sphinx was an ecumenical and taciturn human being that destiny refused to spare. Despite his brilliant success, Merckx had known numerous reversals of fortune. In 1969 while preparing to win the Tour of Italy for the second consecutive time, he found himself excluded as a result of a positive finding from a random drug test, in the Parme-Savone. "I am certain of your innocence, but the results are positive", deplored Professor Genovese, who administered the anti-drug program.

This affair infuriated some and inflamed the controversy because the experts had released the test results without warning the interested party. When Merckx saw Vincent Torriani relating the tale of his "crime" at his hotel it was too late to react.

The Belgian government requested an investigation and even went so far as to threaten to interrupt diplomatic ties with Italy, but to no avail. The deed was done! It was unbearable for the young Brusselian, who quit the ordeal in tears into the arms of his wife, Claudine, after her hurried arrival from Milan.

We will never know the full and true end to this story because it is filled with controversies. There were too many shameful things that went on. Many hypotheses formed were flawed. There was complicity and machination, carried on largely by others. It was no secret. Everyone knew that Merckx enjoyed Italian publicity. It was as ingrained as they were in their lust for world cycling domination. Just the evening before the test, Merckx received a message from Felice Gimondi, who was his rival in the Transalpin, proposing to him (Merckx) that he forego his victory in exchange for a lump sum of money. Some years later Merckx admitted he had asked, "I want to know for sure how much?"

His career could have ended there in the scandal and shame but nothing could tame the religious fervor and visceral love he had for his job. However, after the drug incident we noticed a perceptible change in his attitude. His former ingenuity changed to one of suspicion. The young sprinter, happy in the 1966 race from Rome to San Remo remained in the shadows behind a scowling, unpenetrable, pouting and suspicious human being, who found his comfort in exercising his solitary power.

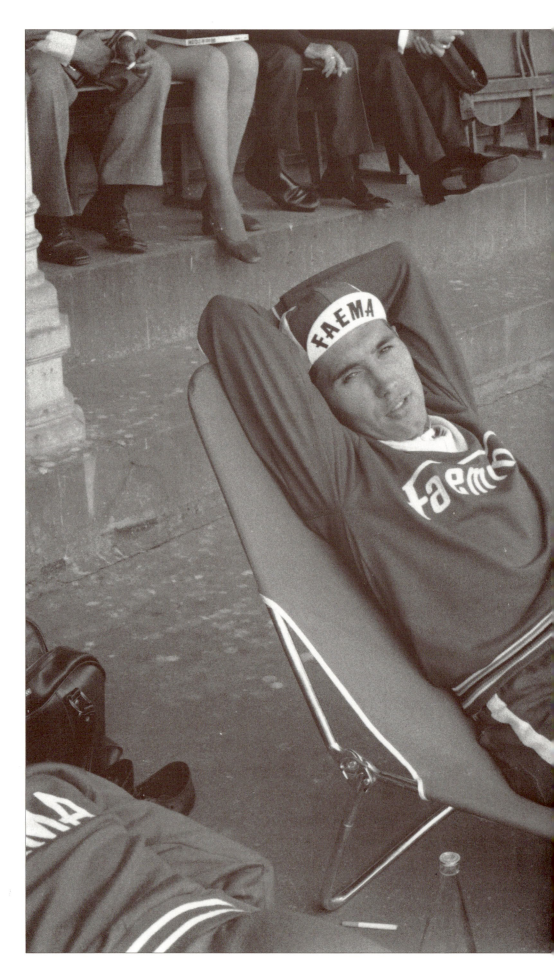

Before the cameras he was affectionate with his wife Claudine, on a day when the Tour was relaxed.

Eddy Merckx already reigned over his racing group, when he won his first Tour in 1969. He was the Amateur World Champion in 1964, then Professional Champion in 1967. He had already won all the trials on the racing calendar: Milan-San Remo, Tour des Flanders, Paris-Roubaix, Liege-Bastogne-Liege, and let's not forget the Tour d'Italy, despite strong opposition from Felice Gimondi, who was the Tour's winner in 1965 and presumed to be the successor to Jacques Anquetil. That mantle was one that Merckx moved quickly to inherit. We know that he excelled in each discipline, including the "Six Jours" (Six

Days). Come winter the excelling Patrick Sercu, his promotional buddy, would wear the green jersey of the Tour de France. Very eclectic, Merckx rivaled the true climbers in the mountains. He feared no sprinter beyond 200 meters. Able to dominate the stopwatch, he felt no pain against cold or heat a fact he amply demonstrated in the famous Trois Cimes de Lavarado, (a top anthology stage of the 1968 Giro) which showed ghostly racers lost in the snow, between the snowdrifts, some hiding under thick blankets mad as hell, others holding on like mad to the doors of cars that were trying to light their

way on the road, and yet others, the most clever, inside the cars thinking they could fool the eye of the race commissioner.

The public ignored nothing about this superb athlete, this son of a grocer, from Woluve-St. Pierre, who was married to a pretty, elegant and discreet woman by the name of Claudine Acou. She was the daughter of Lucien Acou, the ex-director of National Cycling. Not to be overlooked is the fact that Merckx cried over the accidental death of his idol Stan Ockers, or that he owed a lot to his former mentor and old king of the uphill himself, Felicien Vervaecke, who now owned a bicycle

In 1975, he received a sharp blow on the descent of the Puy-de-Dome. At the arrival the Belgian champion was in tremendous pain. His trainer, Guillaume Michiels, helped him to continue the downhill on Clermont-Ferrand.

shop near Laeken, which was the preferred hangout for Brusselian cyclists. It was there that Eddy met Guillaume Michiels, a former racer himself and family friend, who went along on all of Merckx's races, toting suitcases full of bottles and ointments in each hand, always ready to unfold his masseur's table at any given moment to relax the champion's sore muscles, always on his motorcycle and ready to assist in rain or sunshine. Nothing could stop Eddy Merckx in his search for perfection.

Few traces remain of his professional debuts in 1965. At Solo Superia, his friendship with Rik Van Looy came quickly to an end due to discord and resentment. We remember him in revenge on his passage at Peugeot; snubbed by Henri Rabaute in the Giro's uphill; Tom Simpson was his devoted teammate in the Paris-Nice race. (Merckx was the only racer present at the funeral of the Britain in 1967 at the little cemetary in Harmot); beaming from happiness after winning the Heerlen World Championship, where he beat Jan Janssen, Ramon Saez, and Gianni Motta with an interminable sprint.

It is at Peugeot, under the direction of Gaston Plaud and Robert Naye, that Merckx was initiated into the secrets of the big races, stage by stage, at the French bicycing school, which had formerly been the leader in that field. However, it is in Italy, at Faema and under the Molteni tan racing jersey that the Belgian realized all which became essential to his career. At the beginning, Merckx had planned to rejoin Jacques Anquetil under the Ford Team banner, where Raphael Geminiani dreamed of orchestrating a passage witnessing two champions. But Eddy's manager dissuaded him. Jean Van Buggenhout, magnate of the Flemish cycling world and a hard businessman, whose influence

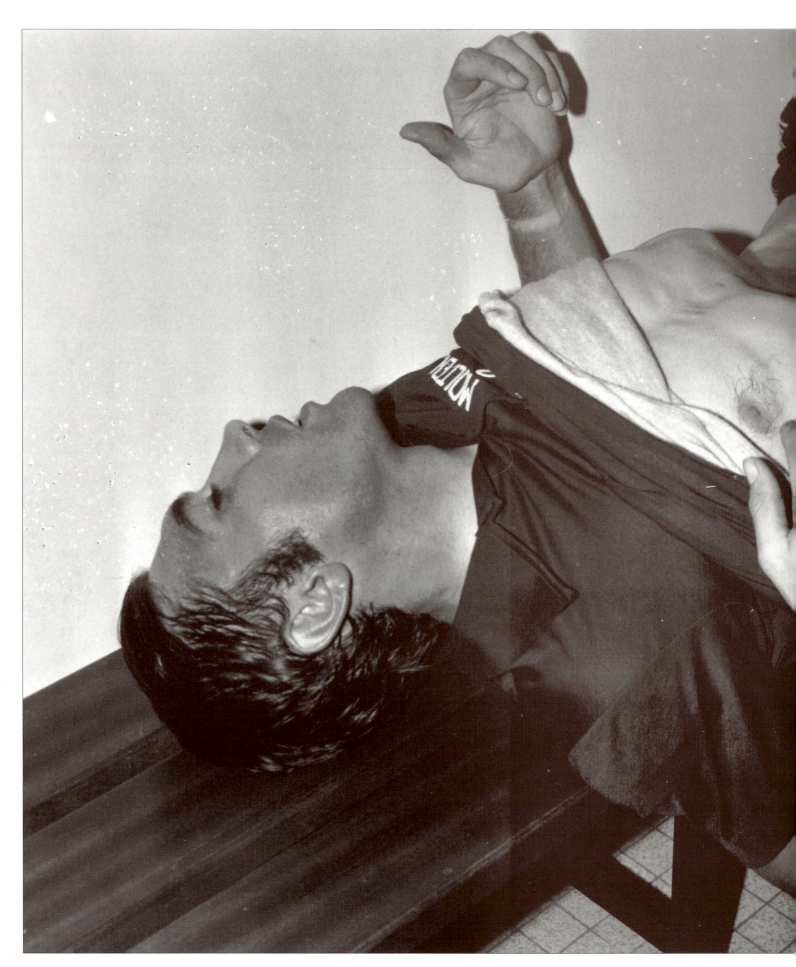

This blow was the most extreme gesture of the anti-Merckxism that raged in France.

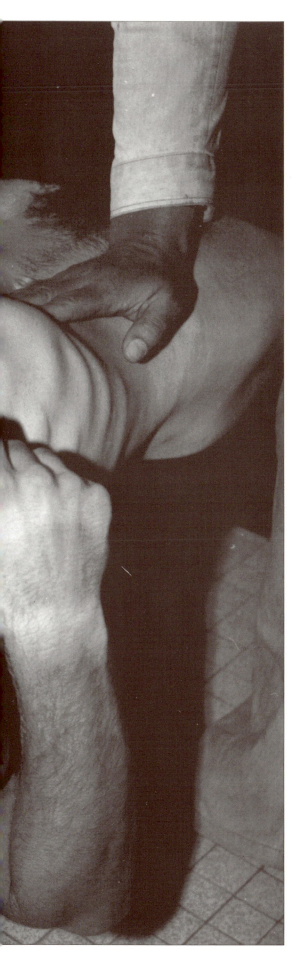

spread to the criterium and the "Six Days" race. He was an accountant by profession- and a former "Six Day man" himself, and he regulated the activities of his colt with an acute intuition of his capabilities, protecting Merckx from himself when he felt it necessary, because Eddy always had the tendency to do too much of what he wanted to do. In 1968 Jean Van Buggenhout understood that Merckx was ready to unleash all his cycling power and was ready to reign as the leader of his group and that Eddy had to be subject to none other than his own authority. It was from this visual idea that Van Buggenhout created the Faema Team, inspired by the system that had been put in place by the legendary Fausto Coppi.

At Faema, Merckx finally could enjoy an entourage entirely devoted to him, a team built around him, attentive, zealous and competent, plus having the technical support of the best Italian parts distributors. He could recruit first class teammates, who were assured of a big salary with a big bonus for victories, generously distributed by Vincenzo Giacotto, its manager. In exchange for all this, these teammates agreed that they would rein in their personal ambitions. Those agreeing to this included: Frans Mintjens, Joseph Huysmans, Victor Van Schil, Joseph Bruyere, Joseph Spruyt, Martin Vandenbossche, and Roger Swerts. It was by this agreement that Merckx was able to find the proper balance, enabling him to win everything that could be won, with the exception of the Paris-Tours race.

Merckx once said, "I didn't have any typical teammates. There was no particular criteria. I refused to have any racers who were even rumored to be on drugs or steroids. I placed importance on spiritual and moral values. Those who are with me must possess an inner sense of the race, knowing when to fan out at the proper moment, when to control the escapes without my intervention. I hate to have to give orders."

He had easily acquired the respect of his "Merckxenaires" and he regularly won his races, refusing to sell out, a practice not uncommon in the cycling world. Gianni Motta and Felice Gimondi tried to corrupt him. The first time was in the Milan-San

Remo race, the second came during the 1971 Mendrisio World Championship. Each time the Belgian replied with a resounding "NO". Sure, there were storms, Big Martin Vandenbossche and Roger Swerts rebelled against his authority. Patrick Sercu slammed the door on the Faema group, because he could no longer support Guillaume Driessens, called "Guillame the Liar" on account of his cynicism. This Driessens was some man. Hired to "sell" Merckx to the press, Driessens was given the role and title of Sports Director, but his arrogance and habit of taking advantage of everything stirred up conflicts and embarrassed Merckx, who did not appreciate this exuberant and tyrannical person, and on top of that, he was always trying to mind his business.

With his team's formation, Merckx multiplied his exploits to the point they became commonplace. He took no less than seven victories in Milan-San Remo, where his genius was expressed without restraint. He won the Tour d'Italy and the Tour de France practically every year, and on October 25, 1972, despite meager preparation, he shattered the old record time of the Dane Ole Ritter. This occurred after an exhausting season, which included a double Giro's -Tour and from diversified success in other races. In 1972, two days after being crucified by Luis Ocana in the uphill stage of d'Orciere, he made a torrid 250 kilometer escape on the oven-hot roads of Provence in the company of Lucien Aimar, Rinus Wagtmans, Joseph Huysmans and Luciano Armani. This group was born in the descent of d'Orciere even though the flag had not yet come down. Merckx presented himself with a reward of two hours ahead of the next best time into Marseilles, where he was surprised by how quiet the town was, not realizing that his arrival time coincided with "siesta" time.

"Who else would try something like that," Luis Ocana said, both astounded by his rival's bravery and furious at having been caught in his trap.

His 1969 Tour de Flanders victory appeared almost too symptomatic of his determination and strong will, which demonstrated his domination to all other groups where rival leaders like Godefroot

After ten years, he held all the cards in his hands.

and Verbeeck in Belgium and Ocana in France had difficulty finding allies. That day there was no opposition. Merckx sprinted ahead under a tormented sky, since he had sixty kilometers to cover and it was mostly uphill. In his wake Guillame Driessens breathed heavily, "...ease up Eddy, please...slow your pace, you will never make it to the end!" Driessens himself did not lack for race experience. He had forced Coppi, when the latter raced in Belgium, he was Rik Van Looy's pygmalion, with whom he built part of Rik's legend. He knew everything about how a champion thinks and also their vulnerability. Driessens ignored the simple fact that Merckx escaped common analysis. "Stop!" Driessens shouted again, "Rain is pouring...it's pure madness". Merckx continued to snub him and outdistance his followers. At Grenbrugge, Felice Gimondi (the Big Gimondi) and winner of the Tour of Giro, plus Paris-Roubaix came in a full five minutes later, and we had to wait more than eight minutes before seeing Marino Bassi and Franco Bitossi, both of whom were unrecognizable. Then came Van Looy, Janssen and Godefroot, fifteen minutes behind! That day there were only 30 escapees. However at the finish line, it was the voice of Driessens who gave strategy lessons to reporters, dumbfounded by so much audacity and relentless persistence as that shown by Merckx.

When he came to his first Tour de France, the Belgian was first in his group, and the press was confounded by his moods, most of which were gloomy. He served as prey to his rivals, who begrudged him his "bulemia", his propensity to gorge down everything, leaving nothing for the others. Regent of a new type, he displayed the same bad temper and the same winning spirit, whether he was racing in a Fleche Wallone, a World Championship or a simple criterium. Victory is a due and it makes for a lot of enmity. "He leaves only crumbs for us," cried his teammates, who nicknamed him "the Cannibal", the name a good racer had dubbed him when sitting at the Peugeot table.

During his long career, observers never stopped predicting for him a shortened career. "At that speed, he won't last long" they said. Before Merckx, the cycling world had not known such an appetite for winning. He was never satisfied with a simple victory. When we saw him speeding toward Mourenx-Ville Nouvell, with a solitary escape of 140 kilometers beyond Aubisque and Tourmalet, admiration took the place of stupor. Merckx had evolved from another planet, prefiguring his destiny like Neil Armstrong's first steps on the moon.

His own legend was born before the myth was solidly established. He started reaching an absolute plane that Coppi, on certain days, had only skirted. We can only ask ourselves where his "Palmares" (list of victories) would be, had it not been for an event two months later on September 9, 1969, where he became victim of a fall on the road to Blois. A fall from which he carried the aftermath for a long, long time. That day, two dernies had telescoped and Fernand Wambts, his trainer, died. Merckx was so deeply affected by those two tragedies that he stayed in bed for three months. Eventually his unshakable belief in himself, which sublimated his destiny, helped him to rebound.

"I began again just like before, but I was unable to find my efficiency in the mountains", he said. "I had displaced my pelvis and I was in constant pain. At vertebrae level the pain was intense and chronic, and my defeat at d'Orcieres was a result of that." September 9, 1969 marked a turning point

in his career. Merckx started to play with his bicycle during the race. We even saw him changing his bicycle seat during a solitary escape, without even loosening his grip on the lead. Searching for a more comfortable position, forced to repress his outgoing nature, he cried out from the pain. In 1970 he entered the Tour d'Italy with no less than eighteen bicycles, which he had pierced, part by part, with a hand drill as testimony to his manic obsession with the weight of his bikes. Then came the first sign of stagnation. In 1971 Georges Pintens rejoined him for the Liege-Bastogne-Liege finale, in which victory was missed by one short breath. In July, Merckx was crucified by Luis Ocana in the d'Orcieres stage. In 1974 Jose Manuel Fuente harassed him during the Tour d'Italy uphill, where Merckx had to dig deep inside himself for his secrets to pull out a win by 12 short seconds ahead of the handsome 20-year-old Italian by the name of Gianbattista Baronchelli. Twelve months later, Merckx is about to win his sixth Tour de France when he receives a severe blow to his liver administered by an agressor right out of the crowd, who was arrested and then released when Merckx refused to press charges. It was in France, with its numerous anti-Merckx manifestations, that the "Cannibal's" success most irked the public.

Eddy Merckx, like those who bask in the public eye, had numerous partisans. After the Savonne affair, he received more than seven thousand letters of support and also some letters from violent detractors, as his reign unleashed as much hate as it did passion. He received threats, taken seriously by the police, forcing him to leave some days under police escort. Some people spit on him, others threw rocks, but no one ever saw him give it back...EVER. However the Puy-de-Dome

incident achieved its goal to undermine Merckx. Just days later Bernard Thevenet overwhelmed him in the Pra-Loup uphill, then Merckx, seemingly with no luck at all on his side, fractured his jawbone when he crashed into the Dane Ole Ritter (his predessor on the record board) just before departure for Vallore. In Paris he finished second and with hurt feelings but more popular than ever. His last triumph in the Via Roma de San Remo in 1976 marked the beginning of his decline. On April 19, 1978 during the evening of the Kermesse de Kemzeke, his healer, Pierrot DeWitt came alongside Merckx. Merckx told him, "You see Pierrot, I just ran my last race." Both men returned home by car. Merckx put an end to his career. DeWitt received the news like he'd been struck with a whip. There was a moment of adjustment, then the healer tried to reason with Merckx, all the while not ignoring the fact that he had passed a rough winter, spoiled by the Fiat team's dissolution. DeWitt advised Eddy to stay calm and not hurry into anything. He developed all kinds of arguments, but the champion was no longer listening. "I was convinced he was not at his end, that he could still shine...at least in the classics, and that he was just going through a bad time and that it would pass, but he felt he just couldn't do it any longer," DeWitt reported. Since the death of Van Buggenhout, Merckx no longer had anyone to advise him and lighten his load. In the car, Eddy was not even sad. He simply did not have the emotional strength to go on any longer.

His return to civilian life was painful. Like an actor dispossessed of his role, Merckx continually found himself confronting his thoughts and they were not very good thoughts at that. He daydreamed that perhaps there was not another life for him after cycling and he

suffered from depression. Unscrupulous businessmen tried to take advantage of his condition. His name was cited in a fiscal fraud deal. It was not difficult for him to plead his case but deep inside he felt dirty. He had just learned about the real world. Claudine's presence plus the affection of his children, Axel and Sabrina, gave him the opportunity to acquire a new balance in his life.

The past forgotten, Merckx created his new bicycle factory and renewed his links within the professional groups.

His son Axel, a member of the Motorola team, attempts today to reclaim the renowned Merckx name. Sixteen years have passed since his retirement and time has not altered the memories, Each year, his ghost holds forth on the banks of Poggio and in the trenches of d'Arenberg. His effigy in bronze stands guard on the coast of Stockeu, a strategic passage point of the Liege-Bastogne-Liege.

We often wonder, in the small world of professional cycling, if he was the century's greatest champion. Let's dare to answer. It is possible that Fausto Coppi had dominated Merckx on certain days in the mountain climbs, and we can reasonably think that Jacques Anquetil could have beaten him against the stopwatch, but there was in Merckx a little of both men, plus something indefinable, like a soul supplement. To that thought, Merckx was Coppi, plus Anquetil and Van Looy. He was, in short, the incarnation of bravery itself.

After him, there was Bernard Hinault, and other champions will come to take the place of Miguel Indurain, the product of a standardized society, team leader of programmed cycling. We will live with other grand Tours, other emotions in the same order, but one question will persist, begging to be answered. That question is: "who will do better than Merckx?"

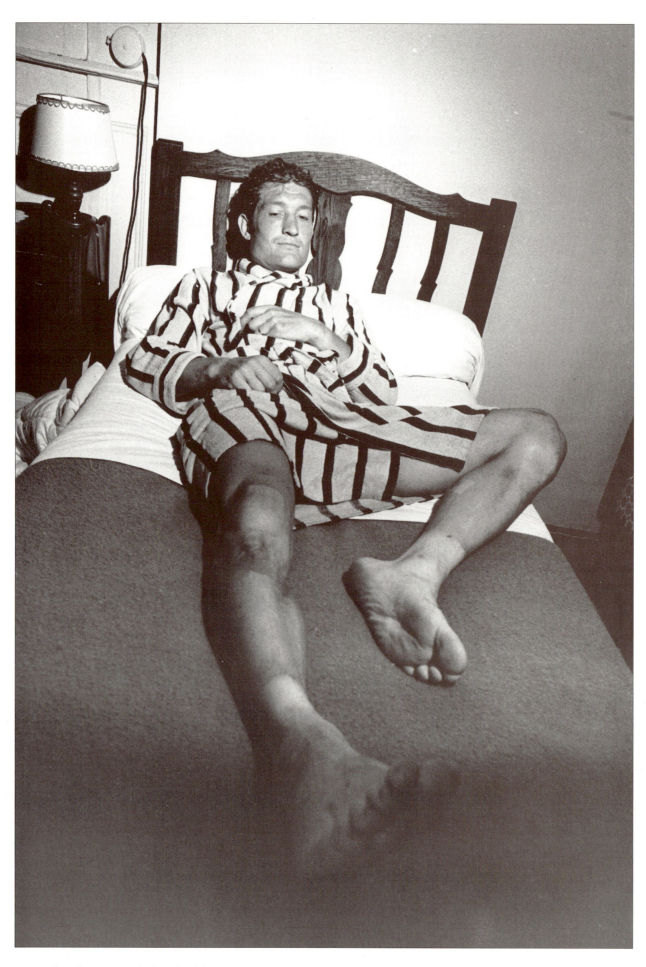

Under the intense light of Eddy Merckx, Cyrille Guimard finally succeeded in having a name for himself.

"Always second", like Poulidor but less popular, Joop Zootemelk was the priviledged adversary
of Bernard Hinault, after having been that of Eddy Merckx.

BERNARD THEVENET

The French surprisingly called him "Nanard" like they would say "Poupou" for Raymond Poulidor. Surprising in that the nickname was at the same time demeaning and grotesque, yet situated Bernard Thevenet at his true place. In the pantheon of popular and familiar champions, the Burgundian had won his place from patience and strong will, and by consistent progress. In the manner of Louison Bobet (both had won the Tour at 28 years old, after five fruitless attempts). Going back a couple of years we can say there was between them a kind of affiliation, which transgressed the moral and the generational gap. The Burgundian (Thevenet) didn't ignore it. Curious about everything, he took time to read autobiographies of champions from after the war, and not having any role model, he accepted the idea that they compared him to the Briton (Bobet). He was flattered.

Son of an agricultural family which ran a farm in the Charolais area, also nick-named "Water bottle", the young Thevenet had crossed progressively the steps to notoriety; in becoming Champion of France Juniors in 1968; finishing 7th in the Tour de l'Avenir (Tour of the Future); and winning the race of the coast of Mont Faron. In his professional debuts, in front of Merckx who was a victim of a fall, and in front of Gimondi and Pingeon. Winner in 1970, under the Mongie's fog on his first participation in the Tour. He took his departure after the resulting forfeiture of

Ferdinand Bracke, he was considered among the outsiders when he was taken, in 1972, in a terrible fall in the company of Alain Santy, Lucien Van Impe and Luis Ocana in the descent of Solour. This episode was the origin of a temporary amnesia.

"I lost the sense of balance, to the point Gaston Plaud and the mechanic had to support me for more than 200 meters before I could start again. Finding my way, I had to climb the thread of my own existence to know who I was, and what I was doing on the bicycle! Then I saw the word 'Peugeot' on my jersey and I remembered that I was a cyclist. But in what race were we? I didn't have any idea, until I noticed the Tour's yellow plate screwed on the bumper of the Peugeot's team car. Not being sure of anything, I am inquiring from Gaston Plaud who answered: 'Yes, we are in the Tour, don't worry, you fell on your head...' I believed I was beginning to slip out, but then a little group came from behind, and in that group, I recognized my teammate Wilfried David. I took advantage to ask him if we had climbed the Aubisque, thinking I was exaggerating, he did not answer, and it wasn't until the sight of the last 20 kilometers on the sign that everything came back in order; the beginning season of the race on the Riviera, the classics of springtime, the Dauphine..."

Placed under observation at Luchon's hospital, Thevenet refused to give up. Four days later, he had won at Ventoux, despite

the emotional shock, then he later relapsed in the Alsace, proof he had resources and courage to spare. Second to Luis Ocana in 1973 (in the absence of Eddy Merckx), affected by a zone in 1974, he entered history the following year, by putting an end to the reign of Eddy Merckx, formerly unconquered in a big race of stages since the 1969 Tour de France. The unlikelihood of unseating Merckx was produced in the 15th stage between Nice and Pra-Loup. Let loose by the Belgian in the uphill climb of Allos, the "Lion Cub" as we called the wearers of Peugeot's checkerboarded white jersey, achieved the stage to suit his rhythm when the race rocketed in the Pra-Loup uphill. Told by spectators of his tardiness which was decreasing, he couldn't believe his eyes when, close to four kilometers of the summit, he stumbled on a barricade of vehicles. A drama was set. Merckx was there, in distress, just in front of him. He was almost stopped and rolled on a band of liquid tar, proof that he did not have all his faculties. The strength of Thevenet increased tenfold. He got up on his pedals and doubled his efforts past the Belgian champion without looking. Three kilometers higher, he put on the yellow jersey, vowing not to take it off again.

That same evening, we learned that Merckx had suffered from a violent pain at the level of the vertebrae, the result of an old fall in the Blois Velodrome, and that in the uphill of the Champs he encouraged his teammate Ward Janssens to take him to

Thevenet on the ground after the descent of Soulor, in 1972; he is temporarily amnesic. It would be many long hours before he regained his mental capabilities.

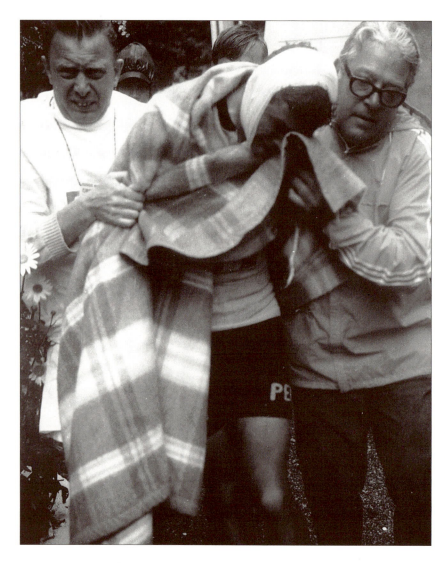

"Oh yes, it is good in the Tour, don't worry, you have fallen on your head..." (Gaston Plaud to Thevenet, Tour de France, 1972).

Dr. Miserez and get some painkillers.

The Tour played on, but in the terms of his homeric stage, full of emotions, we always remark to ourselves about the self control of the Frenchman, as well as his capacity to reassemble his teammates; because Thevenet had often needed to be castigated to obtain his best efficiency. "You go very strong, but you are too often resigned to be second. You have to be more audacious, more ambitious!" repeated Maurice de Muer. Everyone at Peugeot, teammates, sport directors, trainers and mechanics, participated in the psychological conditioning of the Bourguignon, who increased his distances, as early as the day after, between Pra-Loup and Serre-Chevalier. He presented himself alone on the Izoard, after doubling and countering Merckx in the downhill descent going to Vars. "When we had beaten Merckx only one time, nothing stops you," Thevenet declared.

In Paris, Valerie Giscard d'Estaing came to greet him on the Champs Elysees, where the Tour had its final stage for the first time. The day after, his triumph spread across the daily newspapers, and in eight columns *Le Canard* announced that France was in "Nanarchy", an era had ended. His era was achieved two years later when he won a second time in the Tour in front of Hennie Kuiper. During the 1978 winter, Thevenet revealed the usage of dangerous preparations, the base of which were corticoids and anabolics. He was talking about himself, suggesting to have used them. He wanted to testify in order to return to healthier notions, but those claims, done at the hospital bed, were not received well. Some people had judged that for him the revelations came a little late. There were reproachments from peers, and ingratitudes from the cycling circle. Stunned by the "scandal" the house of Peugeot begged him to be taken care of elsewhere.

He took refuge in the heart of a Spanish team, where his presence was regulated to that of an exile. Never again would he play the lead role in the Tour de France.

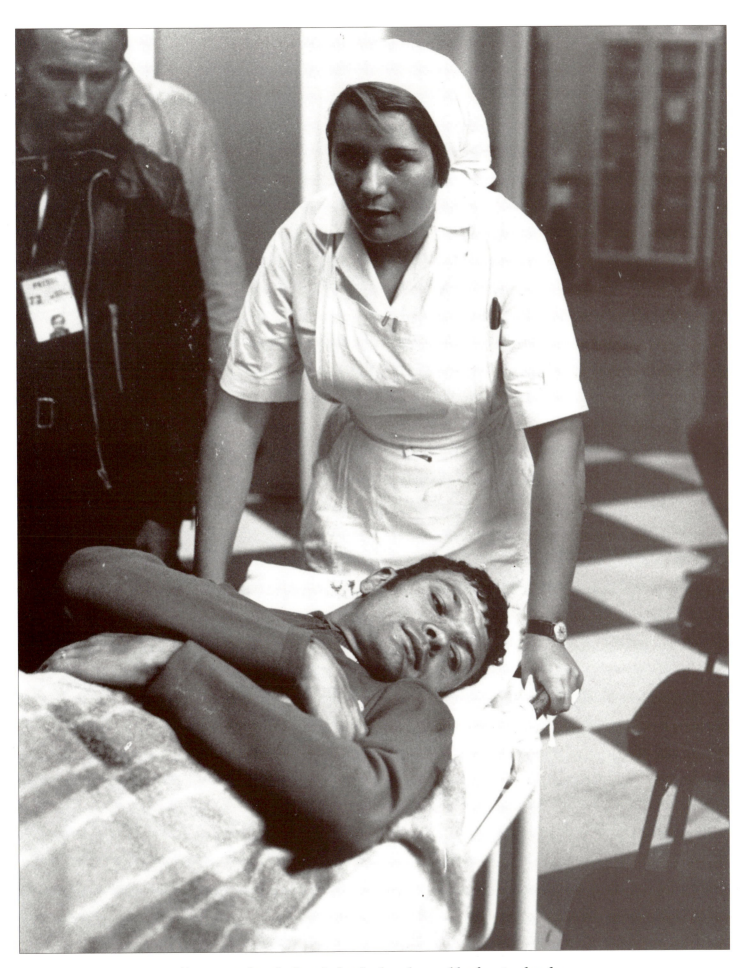

Transported to the hospital at Luchon, he would refuse to abandon.

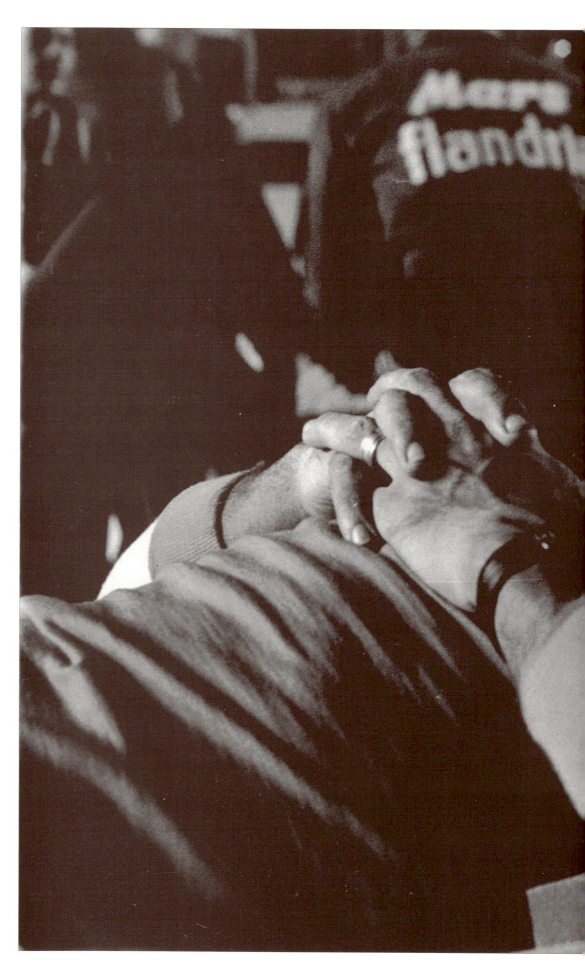

Luis Ocana lost in his dreams.
He had the physique of a
matador. The Tour was his arena.

The petite Spaniard Jose Manuel Fuente had so much heart to share, but his talent would be consummed in the very rough battles he would surrender to the champion Belgian.

Luis Ocana and Jan Janssen: two first-class champions who would never accept folding in front of Merckx.

DIETRICH THURAU

He quit the scene in 1989, with the biggest indifference, far from the desperate and bewildered glances which had welcomed him thirteen years earlier. With time, it was evident that it all would end that way, in the sadness and resentments. Thurau didn't make any efforts to groom his image, to save what it could have been. He let the critics peddle on his account the worst slanders and most ugly rumors, even more, he himself loved to feed them. In 1977, he only needed to speak with Moser outside of the TV cameras, in the World Championship, when he was accused of selling the title to the Italian. Two years later, they suspected him of favoring the hand of the Dutch Jan Raas on the circuit of Valkenburg. We never proved it, but a profound conviction fed the gossip. Dietrich Thurau didn't have the same urgent necessity as Bernard Hinault or Francesco Moser to win races. He preferred only to earn his living, and never lied about it.

Originally from Frankfurt, Dietrich achieved notoriety by wearing the yellow jersey ten days during the 1977 Tour when it crossed the Rhine. The glory he acquired that year never left him, in spite of a meager "palmares" (list of wins). From an obscure role he had voluntarily assumed, in exchange for finances, to race at the side of Giuseppe Saronni, Francesco Moser, and Claude Criquelion. He had all the qualities to succeed, and the physique for cycling, but his cover boy's looks masked a very ambiguous man, at the same time a prince. He was able to seduce both the poor and the aristocrat, and served as window dressing to those who thought that talent should inevitably have a beautiful appearance.

On the hinges of the '80s, he found his place in the Six Jours (Six Days) race, he made his career a seductive business, and soon had only a distant rapport with the younger prodigy. Winner of six stages in the 1976 Vuelta, fifth in the 1977 Tour after crossing the mountain passes in the com-

pany of Thevenet, and Kuiper; the young German presented a devilish and seductive image. Each believed that Dietrich would go on to succeed the King Merckx, but his "prodigal son" image sent him, instead, straight to failure.

Momentarily, Thurau did not appear to be very affected, because youth often encounters failures and pretends to ignore them, but he was already disillusioned when he imposed himself in the Bastogne-Liege, the only classic he had ever won. He already numbered his career path by the deutch mark, but we had to understand him: Thurau was an experienced racer (he was a World Champion), he won in the Six Jours close to 40,000 french francs each evening, and without doubt, he had already acquired the conviction that he would never be rivaled on the road by Bernard Hinault. From Breme to Dortmund, from Munich to Copenhagen, from Grenoble to Anvers, Thurau solicited the public, burning the hardwood floors after burning the stages; abandoning in winter the adulterated velodrome, and the energy which would fail him in the coming summer in the heat of the Tour de France.

"In the Six Jours, racers didn't drug themselves systematically, but they were damaging their health," affirmed a trainer. "They take sleeping or wake-up pills, or even pills to keep their appetite. They ruin their liver and it takes them two or three months to find a rhythm for regular life."

For more than ten years, each winter, the German had endured a strict diet which left him weakened in the Spring classics where he could have made himself very valuable to the reign of De Vlaeminck and Moser on the northern pavements if he had really wanted to.

"While he was wise for not racing in two or three of the Six Jours, he would have made fifteen times as much for racing it," Cyrille Guimard underlined, "but his goal was to make a fortune, and in that he badly managed his time, because without

any doubt, in my eyes, that racer was capable of winning the Tour de France."

Ennobled by wearing the yellow jersey, harassed in every direction of the velodrome, the "beautiful Didi," as we called him at the time, tried to reconcile the irreconcilable, to change without damage from the sunlight of the bicycle path to the sunshine of the grand Tours. He didn't cease to be the show, counting on the idea that you don't judge people by who they are, but more likely judge them for what they suggest. He always went with the best offer, often changing his mind, without any ties binding him. Incapable of blending in with the collective he confided to us one day, "I had to expatriate to exercise my job, either in Italy or Belgium and didn't always find understanding. I endured a discouraging period. It happened that as soon as I announced my retirement, that I contradicted it right away, because I love cycling more than I thought. I thought perhaps I could be at the same height of notoriety as Bernard Hinault if I could enjoy like him, a more quiet atmosphere. If I had a manager by my side, someone who could help me make choices... Myself, I didn't have anyone to stimulate me."

On a strictly sportive plane, there were regrets: "I would love being World Champion," he admitted, "but at San Cristobal, in 1977, Moser had beat me in the sprint because he was stronger than me, and that race, believe me, I didn't sell it. Yes, I sold small races, but a World Championship doesn't have any price. I had an agreement with Moser, who, if he won, had to pay 50,000 deutch marks. He had to race without looking back. He beat me and I received the money, but it doesn't mean that I sold my luck."

In 1980, Konrad Kotter, an ex-baritone from the Opera, converted to the cycling business where, intoxicated by Thurau's charm, he formed a cycling team devoted to him. But the capricious German star, in his selfishness, quickly discouraged his

Thurau is situated in the line of Hugo Koblet, with whom he shared an inalterable distinction. But the German did not have any illusions, during his ten days in the yellow jersey, he indexed his career to make himself more marketable.

mates and his precious boss. Two years later, Thurau was transferred into the heart of the Del Tonga team, which made him pay homage as a support man to back up Saronni. That done, the German had the audacity to reclaim the bonus in the early morning stage of the Dolomites, threatening to quit if his request was not honored.

Expelled from the Tour de France for having accosted a commissioner, he was dropped from the Six Days of Berlin after a strong altercation he had with the organizer, Otto Ziegler. In an attempt at precaution, the German had dug his own grave in the racer's ranks. The business made big news in Germany where "Didi" was forbidden to race in the "Six Jours" for two years. Rejected by the public, chased away from the Munich velodrome for "blackmailing sports and finance," he took his retirement to preserve what little sympathy he still incited.

Months later, interviewed for the weekly magazine *Sport Bild*, the German declared with relief, "My closets now will be empty of syringes and prohibited substances. The majority of racers have resorted to drug products, and those who refuse to admit it, are liars."

He came to expiate his faults. Another life had opened up for him.

Regis Delepine and
Jean-Pierre Danguillaume.
During the '70s their conversa-
tion would invariably turn to
Merckx, for whom the two
Frenchmen had a frank
admiration even though
they were adversaries.

An attempt to control one's destiny is held by an elite few. Bernard Hinault would leave the cycling world in full glory at 32 years of age, the date he himself had fixed.

BERNARD HINAULT

Bernard Hinault quit the team at age 32, on a date he had previously fixed, faithful to this promise as he was with any of his obligations. He did it with pride, not offering the spectacle of his defeat to the "mangy dogs", those "rapacious parasites" (the press) that had for more than ten years, never stopped tracking all his mistakes. They had belittled his language barrier, harping on his neglect of races, with an obstination that would not let up. He refused to give them that pleasure. When he tried to castigate the reporters, Bernard Hinault never had enough words to define the galling emotions which he felt for them. They had to submit to his gloomy moods, and his violent actions, because this man had strong character, and a marked aversion to the press. He never talked about his emotions, but his refusal to work with the press resulted in perverting the image of this super-champion, and it was reflected in public opinion, which reacted to what it read.

When he turned his back on his own legend, Bernard Hinault did it without hesitation or regret. Would he have been nurtured if he had cooperated with them? But what's there to regret anyway? He won everything, well, almost everything, at least all of what he had really wanted to win. He gave himself a 140 kilometer escape in the company of Silvano Contini to win the Lombardy Tour in 1979, and this performance earned him the respect from the Italians ("ad vitam eternam", Live Forever!) The following year, he was transformed into the Knight of the Apocalypse by winning the Bastogne-Liege Tour while racing during a storm. He also became World Champion by crushing all his rivals on the Sallanches circuit. Giving credit where it is

due, it was the press that brought up how he flew in the Stelvio, which allowed him to grab the Giro in 1980; his strong push between Salamanque and Avila in the hell of the Vuelta in 1983; his comeback shattered in the Lombardy Tour in 1984, the day after surgery to his left knee, the same knee that three years earlier, had made him give up the Tour de France. This had to have been a significant decision considering the profound nature of the Breton. He retired not showing his distress in front of the flash of the photographer's camera. "Tomorrow, I'm giving it the boot!" he announced loudly.

As a matter of fact, after leaving, he took refuge at the residence of Hubert Arbes, who was his teammate in the Renault group, and who was eliminated after a fall. At that time, Hinault's five victories in the Tour took second place in his life, probably because he had to wait until 1986, at age 32, to win his first mountain stage in the only Grande Boucle (Great Circle) he was supposed to lose. His yellow jersey was acquired without true opposition. Assured of victory, with his clear advantage against the stopwatch, he faced off against Joop Zoetemelk and Joachim Agostino both of whom were in their thirties. Before leaving the Tour in 1983, to have his knee operated on, he had ruled without having to share his reign for too long a time, on a team under the dictatorship of Eddy Merckx.

Bernard Hinault was a member of the Belgian team, but contrary to Merckx, Hinault dreamed he would last forever. He acted like he was his own boss, snubbing everyone who didn't like his way of running the show, reserving for himself the right to personally reprimand the unruly. We saw him on one

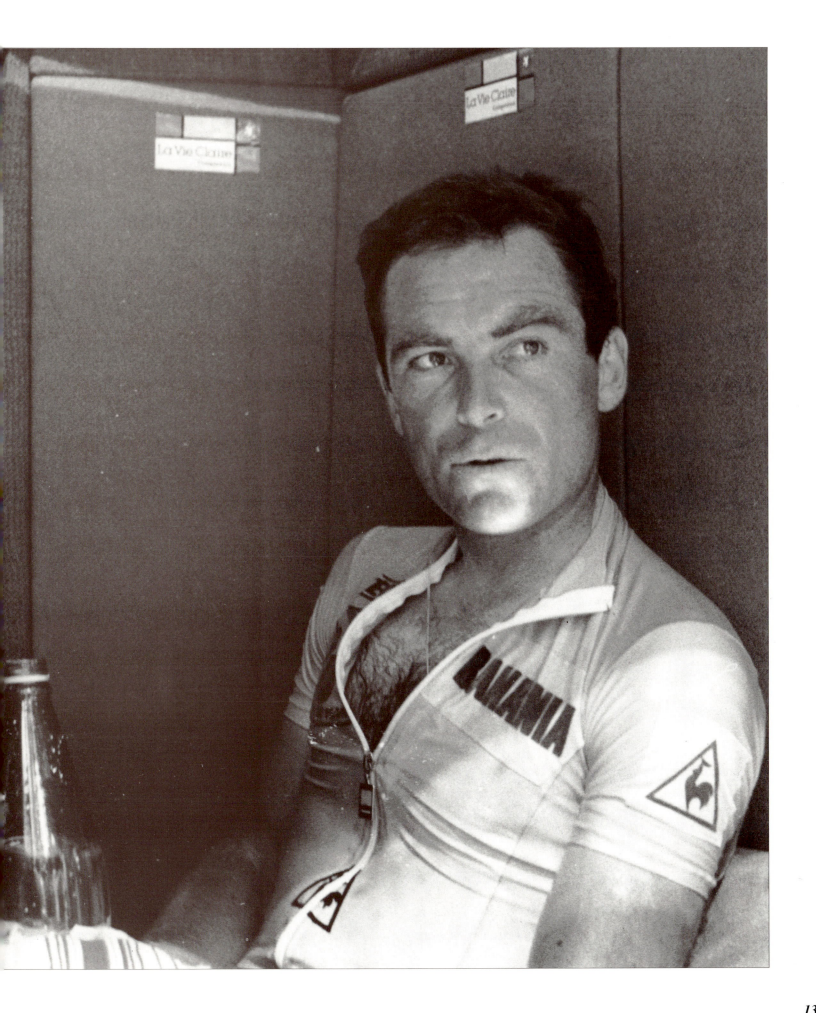

He had the courage of his opinions, but he was not always the best example of them.

occasion threaten the Byzantine Joel Pellier who had the audacity to attack him in the transition stage.

Bernard Hinault was born for action...not diplomacy. He provoked people when he gave his opinion. He denounced the hypocrisy of the World Championship which he disputed according to the national teams' rules. He criticized the Tour de France organizers for allowing Koppenberg to register in the race. He also felt some aversion for the Paris-Roubaix race, which he found too archaic for his taste.

"It's like the Flanders Tour, it's stupid, it's a circus," Hinault said. "There's way too much at risk, what good is it to race there and maybe break bones and have to give up the Tour?"

The truth as always is more of a nuance, because he complained about a race from another time. If he refused to accept Paris-Roubaix as "Queen of the Classics", his sense of defiance suggested that fact. Even though he was always controversial, he did everything he could to win. Twenty-five years, to the day, after Louison Bobet had won Paris-Roubaix,

Hinault won it, swearing that he would not ride it again!

So this is Bernard Hinault, full of rejections, impulses and obsessions. However he was also capable of endorsng ideas other than his own, defending a just cause, or was it because this was the way he had been brought up? In 1978, in his first participation of the Tour de France, he was in the front row when the racers came on foot at Valence d'Algen to demonstrate against the abusive treatment of all transfering racers. During the Paris-Nice Tour, some years later, he shook his fist at a gesturing gentry from Ciotat who had blocked his way on the road.

"No one will ever prevent me from doing my job!" he screamed.

In fact, no one ever did keep Bernard Hinault from being Bernard Hinault, a man without concession, from a modest family, where he was content having little.

"In our house, it was to each his own," Hinault said when asked about his youth. If he never became a national celebrity like the image of the tennis star Yannick Noah, it was because popularity was not a really important issue for him. Glory for

him didn't matter. He looked at his job as a supplemental exultation, refusing to endorse the "giants of the road" myth.

"It's me who is pedaling," he answered to those who incited him to try and break the time record.

He honored his contracts, and always had his business with his employers in order. He had conscience enough to realize "a very beautiful thing" had happened to him when he won the Liege-Bastogne-Liege. He wasn't convinced he deserved so much praise for what he had done.

"Snow, for sure it was snowing, for sure it was cold, but I was paid to pedal," was his comment.

His teammates knew that he had finished the race with fingers so frozen that in the future he had to wear gloves when the temperatures approached freezing.

Merckx was not Merckx anymore, Maertens wasn't himself in April of 1977, when Bernard Hinault is revealed as the surprising winner of the Grand-Welvelgem Tour. Three days later, at the beginning of the Liege-Bastogne-Liege, he decided to confuse those who had come to welcome him after his victory in Flanders. He won with a sprint, in the rain and in front of the Belgian Andre Dierickx. In the space of five days, he took Merckx, Godefroot, De Vlaemick, Raas and Thurau, and in doing so conquered an unlimited territory, without even realizing it.

In France, there was stupor. They now knew that a Breton exists without complexes, capable of imposing himself in the races usually won by the best. Again, we ignored the fact that he possessed a "dimensional star" quality. He raced like no one can race, and climbed the uphill in the company of the true climbers. We also noticed that he had a bad temper, snubbing reporters. He could care less about the current rules of convention.

Fausto Coppi had a soul. He was magnanimous. Jacques Anquetil had style. He was agnostic. Eddy Merckx had nobility. He was religious. Bernard Hinault had vigor and temper.

The French shriveled as they watched him fall in the descent of the col de Porte during the Dauphine-Libre Criterium in 1977. That day, with that accident, he entered into the unconscious collective, because the accident happened directly in front of the TV cameras. Millions of people saw Cyrille Guimard coming to his aid, stretching out his arm to get him out of the ravine. Then they saw the Breton suffer a moment of depression as he thought about the fall. Finally they saw him climbing back on his bicycle and continue the race, with the help of his mechanic's voice, and everybody applauded the birth of a true champion as they watched him impose himself in front of Bernard Thevenet and the little Belgian, Lucien Van Impe, two former winners of the Tour de France.

An epoch was ending. His story was just beginning, and it would be rich in victories in the classics and in the Tours. The Breton gave secondary successes to his teammates, like in the French Championship, where Roland Berland and Pierre Raymond Villemiane knew how to take advantage of his generosity. He was everywhere, and always ready for a fight, rebelling against the press, which treated him badly, not for what he was, but for what they wished him to be. Bernard Hinault was one who split opinions. He could not express himself very well, but he was sincere. At the time when television usurped reputations, he stayed himself, keeping his balance with his wife, Martine, and their two children. He kept to himself as often as possible, and when he came out of his shell, he was always more aggressive on the outside.

In 1983, an accident during the race forced him to give up the Tour. At the Tour d' Espagne he won in pain in front of Lejaretta, Belda, and Gorospe. Hinault had to have his knee operated on. He was torn up inside and announced that he wanted to separate from Cyrille Guimard, his trainer, as relations with the latter deteriorated. At the Vuelta, the two men argued sharply with each other in a restaurant, after Cyrille

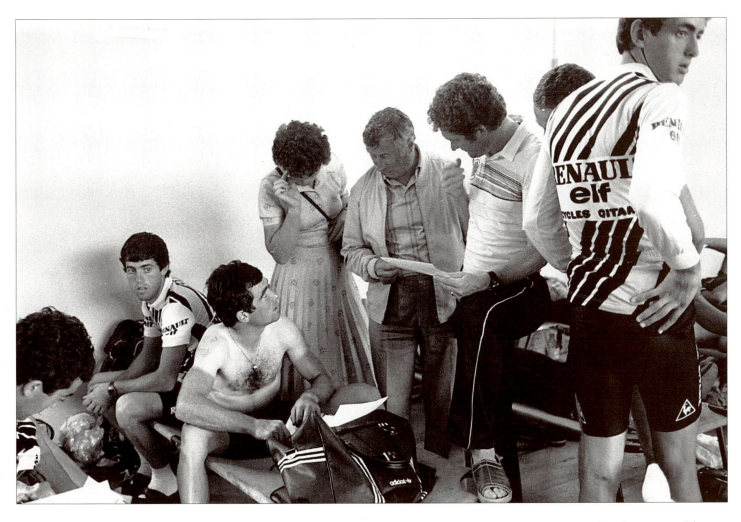

The Breton receives a visit from his parents under the regard of Patrick Bonnet, Cyrille Guimard and Marc Madiot.

Guimard had refused to give him a glass of wine. It was a minor detail, a trifle, but it reflected strongly on the nature of their relationship. Bernard Hinault felt each year, more a stranger to his own training, the heart of which Cyrille Guimard was trying to remodel in depth. He felt like he was being suffocated. "It will be him or me," he told the Renault administration, who then let him go.

In the 1983-1984 winter, the Breton champion was at rock bottom, suffering an unbelievable loneliness, deeply hurt by the action of his former team. He went six months without racing, but something so bad became something so good. When he returned at the beginning of the 1984 season, Hinault was not the same man. The surgeon must have opened his eyes as he had opened his knee. He took extra care to get along with the press, expressing himself in the manner of Raymond Poulidor and even seemed to admit the temporary superiority of his former teammate, Laurent Fignon, who had taken advantage of his absence by winning the Tour de France.

During his recuperation, he looked for a new employer capable of understanding him. He wanted to be his own boss and be associated with a trainer who would listen to his advice on the recruiting of teammates and how to elaborate on his program. He tried it in Italy, but his search brought him back to Bernard Tapie, whom the media was just beginning to know. It was the beginning of a beautiful collaboration, orchestrated by the Swiss, Paul Koechli, under La Vie Claire colors, where each one brought with him a little of the affection that had been missing with the

Renault team, either from indifference or inability.

At the beginning of the 1984 season, Bernard Hinault raced without thinking, with the soul of an amateur in search of a new point of reference, a new goal to push back everyday. At the Dauphine-Libere Criterium, he felt the Colombian Ramirez' law. In the Tour, it was Laurent Fignon who made fun of him at the summit of Alp-D'Huez, after Fignon had easily repelled an attack from the Breton in the Oisans Valley.

"I don't know what it took to make him attack, but for myself, it made me laugh," the Parisian declared.

Hinault was proud, but he had his bullish moments, plus sudden bouts of depression, but he refused to be discouraged, because self-doubt was his worst enemy. He stood up and accepted everything that came his way, without whining, he endured the sarcasm, and the digs about his Tour defeat. Resting within this recuperating man was the germ of great future hopes. He now felt capable of bringing big improvements to the climbs and to produce major efforts against the stopwatch.

At the end of the season that marked his reincarnation, he won blow-by-blow: the Grand Prix des Nations, the Tour of Lombardy, and the Barrocchia's Trophy in the Trente region, associated with Francisco Moser, the latter haloed by his time record. In the following months, Greg LeMond rejoined him at the team La Vie Claire. For this transfer, Bernard Tapie received a payment of one million dollars, payable over three years. It was the sale of the century, and a comfort for Hinault, who in the absence of Laurent Fignon

(who himself had to be operated on for a tendon) refound his number one position in the world of cycling. In 1985, he won the double Giro-Tour, the occasion in which he declared himself ready to help LeMond win the Grande Boucle the following year.

Months later, he fixed his retirement date to be in mid-November of 1986. "I will stop on the day of my 32nd birthday, but before that, why pass up a last victory in the Tour de France or the World Championships." Those words alerted reporters to understand that Hinault had put his services to the efforts of the American. He corrected that by stating "I said I'd help him win the Tour, but on the condition that he honor the yellow jersey."

During the Tour, he forgot his own promise and went deliberately in search of a sixth victory. That's what we all were waiting to see, but what we saw instead was muffled steps. He chose the wrong approach. He attacked between Bayonne and Pau, thus placing LeMond with the moral obligation of protecting his escape. If the American failed to protect the escape, the public would be against him, but has he any choice? He risks losing the Tour if he does. At Pau, where he arrived four minutes ahead, Hinault lied for his own sake: "I attacked because we must make the opponents work," he said. "Today, during the efforts behind me, Greg was able to relax on his wheels." Hinault said pertinently that he had "only one rival and that rival is Greg LeMond." But when he thought he had the race in his hands, he made a mistake of pride. Hinault had come very far, but age was against him and his recuperative powers were no longer

that strong. This time he was unable to reach his goal. The end of the Tour was painful for the La Vie Claire team, separated now into two distinct camps, the most numerous placing themselves in Hinault's services. Most of the time Greg LeMond preferred eating alone in his hotel room where his wife and father had come to join him. Hinault felt attacked by the press, menaced by the public and betrayed by Bernard Tapie, who double-crossed him behind his back. At the end, teacher and student united and together ran the uphill of Alp-d'Huez where LeMond took the win and outraged Hinault, who was unable to forgive him for it.

Bernard Hinault's retirement has not allowed him enough time to appease his rancor. The Breton chose to leave in glory, to be out of the terrible seduction of destruction that Merckx and Coppi had encountered. Hinault wanted to be stronger than any human being, stronger than the events and those feelings which had made him at times very arrogant.

Beyond that, he was like any other man.

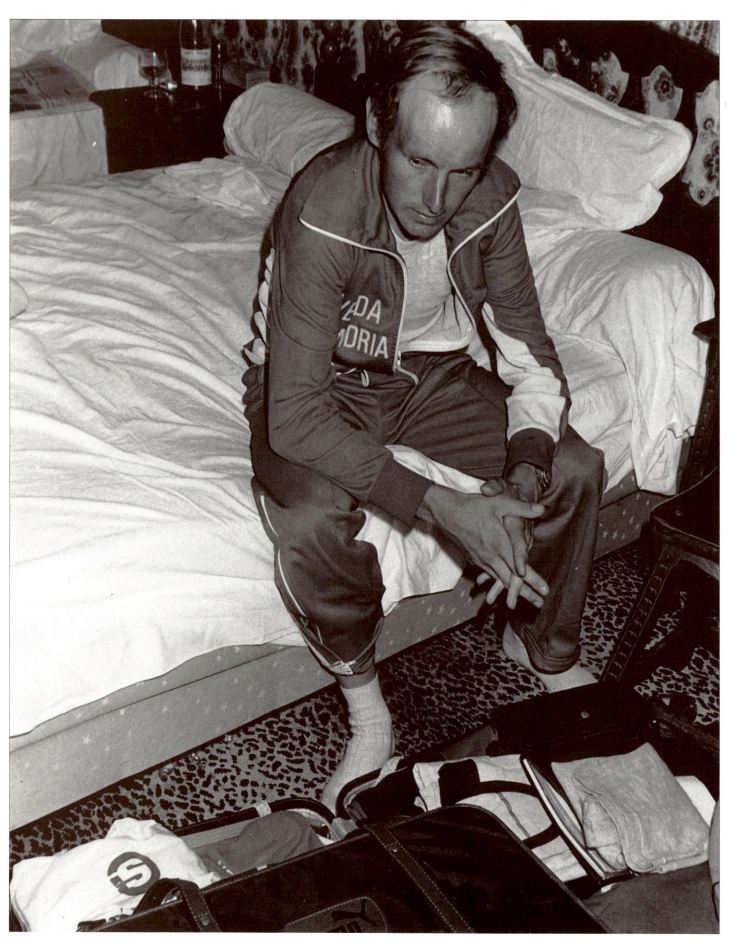

More than 300,000 people came to cheer him on in the Alpe-d'Huez before learning he had cheated in the anti-dopage program. A diverse move without precedent; it would throw discredit on a very good racer.

MICHEL POLLENTIER

With his ridiculous posture gleaned from his arthritis, his thin knock-kneed legs grooved with varicose veins, his morbid paleness and his bald head, Michel Pollentier had the look of a fledgling just fallen from the nest. Bernard Hinault nicknamed him "Polio" (without malice, I might add), and experts found it amusing to calculate the extra kilometers he covered in a race, zig-zagging all over the place. The fact that he had disgraceful speed plus little knowledge of race academics, did not stop him from reaching the sublime by beating the big star Eddy Merckx in 1974 at Orleans against the stopwatch of the Tour de France. In an instant this exploit was greeted like a simple avatar from history. The Flemish was already placed under the tutelage of Freddy Maertens, a cyclist more gifted than he. It was not a disagreement to Pollentier's life, which would affirm his exceptional uphill talents the following year. Seventh in the 1974 Tour de France, and seventh in 1976, his destiny seemed etched in advance for him, when in 1977 Freddy Maertens left the Giro on a stretcher after crashing into Van Linden on the Mugello's Circuit. Pollentier is second in the general classification, less than one minute behind Francesco Moser, and for the very first time was free of servitude. His first reflex was to quit. He told his wife by phone, "what's the point in continuing, if Freddy is not there?"

His Sports Director, the old World Champion Brik Schotte convinced him to continue the race, and it was the beginning of a metamorphosis. The chrysalis was changing into a butterfly. Pollentier took the pink jersey, resisting Gianbattista Baronchelli's pressure in the crossing of the Dolomites. Then he imposed himself, averaging more than 48 kilometers an hour

in the last chronometered race, on the Binago Circuit. His impulsiveness resulted in his actually winning the Swiss Tour by wearing the leader's jersey from one end of the race to the other. He won the Belgian Championship with flying colors, attracting the displeasure of Eddy Merckx, who was in the process of his recuperation.

At the beginning of the 1978 Tour de France, the Belgian is at the peak form of his career. He now had the confidence to fight against Bernard Hinault in the chronometered stages and felt capable of extending it beyond the mountains. He waited for his hour and his hour chimed at the summit of Alp D'Huez, where he put on the yellow jersey after disposing of the Breton in the uphill of Luitel.

Two hours later there is dismay for Pollentier, in front of the drug check control point, where the Belgian was caught red-handed cheating. Here are the facts: having satisfied protocol obligations, Pollentier rode his bike back to his hotel in order to circulate through the conjested streets faster. It was four o'clock in the afternoon. In the privacy of his bedroom, he begins putting on a device which will permit him to furnish a urine specimen not his own. Pollentier is not the only one engaged in this activity. The device consisted of a rubber bulb, full of urine, which was placed under the armpit. The bulb was attached to a tube which ran down his back and under the penis, and was secured in place by adhesive tape. He took a nonsensical risk, but nonetheless took it in good conscience, convinced like so many others that he could fool the doctor on duty.

Since Leiden, racers remarked to each other that the "checkers" were given to a certain benevolence. The word was

passed from racer to racer. Unfortunately for Pollentier, Dr. Calvez, on his first assignment in this area and harried by race officials had decided well in advance to follow all the rules, and he asked each selected racer to give the specimen in front of him, pants down, jersey and sleeves up...measures that had been neglected before.

At six o'clock, Pollentier was ready to furnish one-third of the required amount of urine by applying simple pressure to the armpit, when the hoax was discovered by the doctor. Leaving the caravan one hour after coming in and in the company of Fred de Bruyne, the Belgian displayed a baffled look. He tried to explain the reason it took him so long to urinate. "I put out such effort in the Alp d'Huez, I peed my pants while still on my bicycle, then this evening I had a hard time to fill up the bottle."

We know later that his hand had been caught in the cookie jar and his fraud, pure and simple, caused his expulsion from the Tour. In Belgium where emotions ran high, some observers were for the testing and others against it. In an open letter to Pollentier, *La Derniere Heure* (The Last Hour) newspaper of Brussels heaped deep bitterness and shame upon him for betraying the national cause. "You destroyed Joseph Bruyere, who during the whole day, fought courageously for the jersey that you have disgraced. You have played out a comedy of bad taste, betrayed your teammates and the public."

La Nouvelle Gazette stated, "This story is missing some clarity," and went on to beg the Flanders Team not to remain with a testing system which appeared so biased against foreign racers. Roger Pierre Turine wrote, "That day the doctor changed the method of operation. It is no longer a simple service anymore but has become a watchdog operating with moral support from the public, then 'oops subito presto', pants down and an inspection from armpit to testicles, reducing a person's status and sending him back to mediocrity. Pollentier was sold out. He could not be allowed to win the Tour and that's the end of it."

In the *L'Equipe* columns Jacques Goddet put the situation on a philosophical plane: "We would all like the sport of cycling to stay exempt from dishonest actions which fill up the pages of newspapers." He went on to arouse the avidity with which we voluntarily celebrate the reason and the outcome. "It is upsetting to see an athlete go beyond the limits, but here we are, we reporters singing the praise of those transcended athletes, who have done exactly that. With Pollentier, I don't deplore being deceived by one competitor who cheated. It's worse than that. I am depressed thinking his actions on the cycling circuit which so enthused me and millions of other fans may have come about with the help of forbidden means."

The day after, Pollentier sent a letter of apology to race organizers, begging their clemency. "Despite appearances, I have neither the soul nor the mentality of a cheater," he wrote in his letter. He went on to remind them that his career was like that of other racers, blemished by troubles of 'drug use' and underlined that his 'anxiety' explained it. He concluded "you know enough about cycling circles to

Pollentier was content to be in the shadow of Freddy Maertens, the controversial champion and two-time wearer of the green jersey of the Tour de France.

understand that the ones who are penalized are not the biggest culprits."

Michel Pollentier was not given a second chance. He had acted blindly, in the heat of battle so to speak, without evaluating the consequences of his actions, and no doubt with the back up of some members of his entourage. That same evening, in the company of intimate friends, he told them of his surprise with genuine candor. "I don't understand it, I always use that bulb, and until now nothing had ever hap-pened to me," he admitted.

He even suggested that those doing the checking did not always offer the necessary seriousness, and cast out suspicion on the medical service itself, while recognizing explicitly that his preceding victories would now become suspect.

Pollentier had lost "big time" in the cycling world, which evicted him from the Criterium. Time had done its job.

He reappeared from the darkness to win the 1980 Tour de Flanders in front of two "Big Guns," namely Francesco Moser and Jan Raas, the latter wearing the rainbow jersey captured in Walkenburg, where everyone saw Jan Raas' teammates boost him up in the repeated uphill of Caulberg.

Michel Pollentier left cycling without a roar, much the same way he entered it, in the cold and with his friend Freddy Maertens, both humbled by the brutal death of their friend Marc Demeyer, who had fallen victim to a heart attack.

LeMond-Hinault, the student faces his teacher. Their relations were passionate, often to the benefit of the Tour.

LAURENT FIGNON

He could have raced in the Oslo World Championships, retire in front of Eurovision TV cameras, signifying his retirement by a sadness with a theatrical sharp sense; but it was at Plouay, a little community of Morbihan, far from the big news centers, that he chose on August 23, 1993 to say farewell. Reasons for which Laurent Fignon quit the job, far from the usual ceremony, remain clouded by his character, unclassified and refined. He had a great weariness, without doubt, and the feeling of having demanded too much of himself for too long a time. For one or two years he had seemed vacant, deserted by everything which formerly made him advanced, probably conscious of having been the fruit of an overly-completed era. Those who surrounded him knew that he would refuse to play the game. "I will leave when I do not win races anymore," he said. He kept his word. His retreat didn't leave people indifferent. Radios and televisions gave him a vibrant homage, returning Fignon to his true place, first place, the one which in fact he never left.

"I leave without bitterness or regret," he said sadly. He was at the end of his rope, at the threshold of his new life, like an actor without a role. With him French cycling lost a group leader, a leader in a true sense of the term, a marvelous ambassador, an elegant man, who was misunderstood even when he shared the blame in the conflicts and the misunderstandings which governed his relations with the press and the public.

Laurent Fignon was not like any of his predecessors: in him, it was some of Bobet, nothing of Anquetil. He took the the charm away from its precarious familiarity with the current cycling circle world, and it had to be when he lost the Tour by eight short seconds in 1989, crucified on the Champs Elysees. It was then that the public decided to take him as he was: an honest champion, who didn't do anything to be popular or to maintain with reporters a complicity which he knew to be superficial or false.

He preferred to displease rather than deny his positions. We saw him crash on the Spanish television, and fight with a conceited reporter. Having enemies didn't frighten him, on the contrary, he was there for that. "We can't please everybody," he said. In most circumstances he tended to remain himself, without arrangement, or compromise of any kind, and it was that way until the end of his career. His notoriety was on the road, in the Tour uphill, under rain or heat; it was there that he had wanted to build his career. The remainder seemed to be attainable

"He learned to express himself on the university bench, and his language was not intended to seduce the man of the street," Cyrille Guimard, his sports director said. "Laurent didn't like the crowds, the fans' familiarity made him uncomfortable. He was a real champion, proud to be loved, but a champion aside, not made for this type."

The Parisien was reticent, but didn't fear to express himself when his honor was on the line, or to defend his profession. Strong-principled, he refused to race for a discount (the reason why he didn't participate in the last Criterium), and never lost an occasion to underline the incoherence of the anti-drug controls; affirming his personality on the road as soon as he felt the urgency or necessity to do so.

An innovator in some fields, he was the first to risk his ranking by using some of the most sophisticated materials on his bicycle, but he kept to traditional methods when it came to training, because he was at the same time modern and rational. He evolved during a period of great change, at the forefront of the movement which drove the bicycling world to the highest techniques. There was a total anarchy most of the time which for him translated into two resounding defeats: in the 1984 Giro where Francesco Moser was the only one to benefit from lenticular wheels, and in the 1989 Tour, when LeMond outdistanced him by only eight seconds, in part from the advantages of a triathlete handlebar.

He missed nothing, neither the happiness nor the resentments which are usual in his profession. In 1982, he broke his bicycle pedal at the Chaville entrance, when he was ready to win his first big national classic, only months after joining the Renault team. The following year, he won his first Tour de France at the age of 23, in Bernard Hinault's absence; it was the only time where fate had given in to his destiny. Subsequent to that event, many blond children began to imitate his manner and his schoolboy look. Then in 1985, it was at a high point of his power and fame when he had to have a damaged ligament operated on by Professor Saillant. It was heartbreaking. He resurfaced in 1989, by imposing himself for the second time in Milan-San Remo. That year, he also won the Giro, ahead of Flavio Giupponi, and the Grand Prix des Nations, but public opinion was already set after his defeat in the Tour de France. With very little distance between racers, it was Gred LeMond with his "black beast" bicycle who beat him again on the stage of the Chambery World Championship theatre.

Little by little, he entered into our imagination. After he had broken his bicycle pedal on the pavement, Laurent Fignon celebrated the alliance of grace and fatality, but again his bad luck genie set out to destroy what the athlete had patiently built. In 1990, he pushed the Paris-Roubaix race when he charged five times flat out on the pavements. There was also the brutal death of his childhood friend, Pascal Jules, his accomplice, with whom he had entered the amateurs class; a tumultous and broken relationship with Cyrille Guimard, which he regretted later, but it was too late; and then his golden exile at Team Gatorade in Italy.

His love of cycling had spoiled for him the 1984 Giro, before putting him on the pedestal the evening of his second victory in the Primavera. Nicknamed "Spell" by experts because of his ability to take advantage of circumstances, he was artfully subtle in handling his opponents. Yet he was never able to establish a true alliance with Gianni Bugno, whose failure aggravated his own disenchantment. Often contradicted in his methods, he deployed a phenomenal courage where others would have let go. The man never gave up, but he will never again be the absolute dominator he was in the 1984 Tour, when experts recalled memories of Eddy Merckx and Fausto Coppi to measure the dimension of his class and of his brilliance.

In the passionate years of the '80s he offered an alternative to those who did not appreciate Bernard Hinault's "character".

Fignon was elusive and distinguished, without being conceited. Hinault was a bragger and a fussy guy. Between those two, there was a teacher-student relationship, each familiar with practicing the offensive to excess. A deep respect for one another eventually transpired, transgressing their age difference. Taking advantage of the situation, the press did not help to make them closer, on the contrary, it stirred up passions in an attempt to resurrect the mythic rivalry between Anquetil and Poulidor, for whom there remained a great nostalgia. The press easily opined that Laurent Fignon was an iconoclast, reluctant to be cautious in the conforming atmosphere. He made fun of Bernard Hinault, and refused to give the right to Merckx to judge him; it was said he was not in tune with the world, which doesn't seem quite right, as he often was seen relaxed and his earnings were very good.

"This job brought me a lot, except on the intellectual level, where I felt I regressed, and that was my biggest sacrifice," he confided one day.

His last victory was obtained in the Tour of Mexico, far from his home base, in an anonymous region. He had tremendous style and character, and in his own way, he remains an example of a true champion.

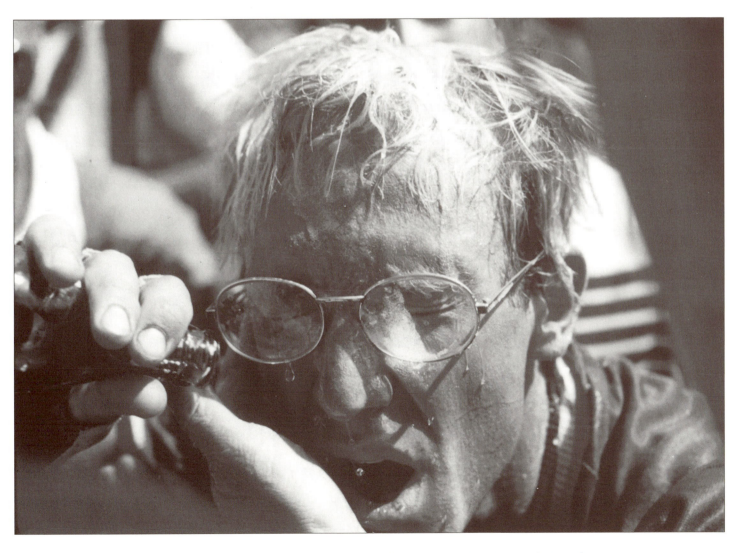

He offered an alternative to those who did not appreciate Bernard Hinault.

1983-1984: Two seasons were sufficient to reap the fruits of his labors. He was just 23 years old when he won his first Tour de France.

CLAUDIO CHIAPPUCCI

Everywhere he went, he unleashed an hysterical scene. Everytime there was a riot, it was the same story. The boisterous crowd just wanted a gesture, an autograph, a word, and the obliging Claudio answered them with smiles and a wave. His kindness was disarming, but this hectic and loud delirium reinforced his convictions that it was for the public he was racing as well as for himself.

"He's the Bartali of the poor," former champion Dino Zandegu said of Claudio. "He may be less spiritual than the Gino of old, but he is just as much wedded to his job, and like Gino, he belongs to the people and gives to the people."

Claudio Chiappucci never refused anything or anybody. Better, he multiplied the signs of friendship and complicity with his fans. The resulting "Chiappuccimania" touched all ranks of Italian society. Additionally, with Miguel Indurain's retirement from the Spanish races, "Chiappuccimania" spread to that country as well. The French idolized him to the point that they included him in most of their criteriums. It spread across the Atlantic to Columbia, where he was called "Il Diablo". Of all the nicknames given to him in his baroque and tumultuous champion's life, this was the one he preferred because it was appropriate for his eruptive nature and presented the idea that he hovered as a menacing and unforseeable shadow over Miguel Indurain and Tony Rominger, the two favorites at the time.

"They should not have too many Romingers," he declared in a sharp tone. "That kind of guy gives the impression that he is just out there doing his job. For me, it is a passion. When I stop, I will be proud to have served and glorified the sport of bicycle racing." Then he added, "My biggest fear is that they will confuse me with another racer."

Not to worry on that score, but how to justify the infatuation he incited? His "palmares" are so slim: winner of the Milan-San Remo in 1991, and a collection of stage races at Sestrieres; tracing Coppi's footsteps in the 1992 Tour de France, he was a specialist in the secondary races.

"Since he first showed himself in the Tour, facing Greg LeMond in 1990, he rarely came out the winner of a big battle, but he continued to be the cause of numerous skirmishes as fantasy faced reality," reporter Claudio Gregario wrote. "Unless under exceptional circumstances, the Carrera team leader will never win the Giro, nor the Tour, but he exists beyond those results. He lives where time has been charged with imposing his image on the public."

It was the image of a generous champion, who never cheated, exuberant without complexes, a practicing catholic. He was from Juve and like Platini, Roberto Baggio and Toto Schilacci, he liked to say, "In Italy, being from Juve is like having an inherited illness." Like a good Italian he loved sports cars and the pasta his mother Renata prepared. He called her everyday no matter where he was, asking how things were going at home, and how is Rita and Giovanni, his older brother, a railroad employee, who was living with them.

"I won less often than Fondriest, but when I win it's historic," he said.

Chiappucci raced for the glory, and was unique in that account. He took risks and the public loved him for it. It's what made him sublime or pathetic, nothing in between. A phenomenon identical to Poulidor, he was, however, less bold. Like Poulidor, the Italian from the Carrera team knew to build his fame on his own failures which were perceived as victories, because he incarnated a new kind of hero, idealistic and courageous and particularly the racer least prone to vice.

"Staying on his wheels is status for him," underlined Mari Fossati, cycling historian of the Transalpin race. His frank and sincere personality upset all those who refused to believe that Italy was no more than a profane and religious den fit only for the mafia and wormy politicians.

Chiappucci acted from his heart, guided by his humor, which was often rebellious. He endured the freezing cold, or strong heat, and his massive and well put-together silhouette evoked the cannonized era of the "convicts of the road". On the opposite side of him was Gianni Bugno, who abhored conflicts and played the role of the frightened one, who enjoyed being nourished by controversy.

At the time of Chiappucci's splendor, not a day passed without him accusing one of his rivals with all kinds of words. He got mad at Pedro Delgado; and managed to openly fight with Moreno Argentin, whom he struck with an open hand over a story about bonuses. We saw him carry on an argument with Mariano Piccoli, a modest uphill racer, who had the audacity to defy him in the mountains of the Trentin Tour. Davide Boifava, his sports director, regretted having him on the team: "To win races, you have to cultivate friendships. Claudio is too impuslive, not enough of a diplomat for that.

The Italian got his temper from -- you know who -- Arduinio, his father, who had served in Ethiopia with Fausto Coppi, and was called "Guerra" because of his resemblence to Learco Guerra, nicknamed "the Human Locomotive", and who had been a champion in the '30s. Arduinio was a robust and frank man, like his wife, Renata, a character in her own right, who pulled the heavy cart to the Varese market to sell undergarments. The Chiappuccis lived to assure the well-being of their three sons, Giovanni, Emilio and Claudio, the latter of whom received his first bicycle at the age of 13. A blue Monti bicycle. One year later, he signed his first license to race at Saronnese, before being transferred to the Cesano Bascone club which was managed by Enrico Maggioni, a former Merckx support rider, and who had also supported Boifavia at team Molteni. As an amateur,

Chiappucci won thirty races, two of which were the Italian Championship at San Rufo, in the province of Salerno; and the Brianza Tour where Dino Zandegu noticed him.

"At the time, I often looked for future prospects in the amateurs races, because I manage a professional group, and I was very impressed by the way Chiappucci imposed himself in front of strangers, in the manner of Merckx," said Zandegu. Later on, some believed it was a last-minute affirmation in turning him from an amateur to a professional that proved to be a miracle. That view totally underestimates the person. Simply put, it takes a long time to produce a champion.

"Chiappa", as they called him then, was still immature when he became professional in 1985 at Carrera. He was muscular with powerful legs, but he was too heavy. "He was regularly passed in the uphill," recalled his old teammate Accaci Da Silva. "He was in the shadow of Roche, Visentini and Botempi and myself, and we were winning the races; and he washed my cycling shorts without balking, because "Chiappa" never balked at anything, until one day, he told me: 'I am tired of washing your cycling shorts! I am going to burn them!' It was hard to believe, but it was that kind of determination in him that immediately convinced me that he would be successful. His debut was spoiled by an accident in the 1987 Swiss Tour which nearly ruined his career. He negotiated a tight descent at the exit of Porrentruy when a driver in the opposite lane crashed into him and Giancarlo Perini."

"I believed he was dead," Davide Boifavia said later. The Lombardian lay unconscious, with a broken leg in a pool of blood. Professor Tabliabue, Tomba's (the skier) personal doctor, operated on "Chiappa", but his condition was guarded, his prognosis so poor that Stephen Roche had to personally intervene with the Carrera administration in order for them to keep him among their personnel. The stubbornness that Chiappucci developed during the long weeks of rehabilitation in the Sereno swimming pool increased his aggressiveness. Other events matured him, the death of his father, who gave him the responsibility of being in charge of the family, and his engagement to Rita, who later bore him a daughter.

The decline of Stephen Roche and the anticipated retirement of Roberto Visentini boosted him to the front of the cycling scene. But at his retirement from the sport, he was measured by what he had never ceased to be: a fantastic explosive, one who always fought to escape the monotonous.

He did not win often, but without him, the Tour lost a little of its bohemianism.

Miguel Indurain and Jose Miguel Echavarri. This plane for them.

MIGUEL INDURAIN

Some called him Miguel, others "Miguelon", giving the illusion of a certain friendship, but it was familiarity only for that day to be welded with the Navarrese and the enamored crowd, hysterical on some days, clammoring everytime for more warmth from him, this "prodigal son" from Navarre. His sports director and spiritual father, Jose Miguel Echavarri, called him "Mystery" pronounced in Spanish as "Mistere", and it was very appropriate...because Indurain remained an enigma, an unknown. Nothing escaped the reporters who loved to follow a man like Miguel, but who can really claim to know him? Who can interpret him? Finally, who can approach him and ask what he is hiding in his silence and disarming smile?

His four (now five) years in power and overexposure did not put a light on that obscure person, difficult to grasp, despite the numerous interviews he gave, but without enthusiasm. He was always polite, because in the champion's ambivalence he was both available and discreet, he gives, but never reveals himself. When his Spanish colleagues speak of their compatriot, it is to confess their inability to explore his psyche, to separate the man from the champion. "Does his wife know who is sleeping beside her?", one of them said with irony.

In eight years of his career, we saw him angry only once. It was in the Giro against Raiman, a certain Salvi who joyfully provoked Indurain by taking the air out of his tires. Indurain then grabbed the camera from the technician's hands, breaking it on the pavement. Another time, he revolted against a paparazzi who had come to spy on his honeymoon trip to Orlando. Outside of these two incidents, the Spaniard kept control of his emotions.

If he hardly spoke, it was also a way to express himself, to confess that he was careful with words, their hidden meanings and their possible interpretations. We often forget that he came from a region with strong traditions, where unemployment was very high, and cultural aspirations were often repressed. In the Basque country, words are weighed with other weights. Was the Navarrese champion afraid he would shock us with his words? "I am Navarrese with a Spanish passport, and my job forced me to feel like an European citizen," he liked to declare, comforting those who pretended that the problem of his own identity was far from being solved.

"If he doesn't express clearly his thoughts, it is because in Spain it is dangerous when you are a public person to do so," explained Miguel Angel Bastenier, vice president of El Pais. "It was also known that the majority of the Navarrese were in Franco's troops. There were no Catholics or Centralists more intense than the Navarrese. Miguel inherited from his parents and grandparents his sensitivity, his cautiousness, and on top of that, he is married to a Basque."

Before asserting himself to be the best cycling racer of his generation, Miguel stayed in Pedro Delgado's shadow, giving the latter six years of servitude without balking. Six years of pure abstraction, leaving nothing, or almost nothing, despite an ephemeral victory in the first European Community Tour, so dear to the heart of Jacques Delors.

He weighed ten kilos (20 pounds) more than he does today, and nobody could believe that the cycling world had hatched such a phenomenom. Such a successor is only born once in a decade. Miguel was Jacques Anquetil's and Bernard Hinault's successor. By association with Delgado, Indurain learned the significance of the words "intoxication," "pressure" and "psychological war", and what event the press was indulged in during the month of July; he wasn't flustered, but we know why. It is in his nature and mentality not to hurry things. In the light of his fourth Tour de France, the question was raised as "how is it possible for Indurain to stay so long in the trail of Delgado?" Here we reach to the mystery of the metamorphosis, to that marvelous alchemy which makes a champion fully bloom, or, to the contrary, take comfort in the cozy darkness of mediocrity, because it is in the end, easier to be a teammate than to be a team leader.

"Miguel is a slow person," said Jose Miguel Echavarri, the man who knows him best. In 1985, to prepare for his debut in the Tour, Echavarri asked him to give up after the Pyrenees' Tour. "Miguel Indurain took time learning to become a man, because in him everything had to be connected. He had to be sure of his strength and balance before he could show his talent in full force," said Echavarri.

The sports director never sought to force the indolent and peaceful nature of his protege. He preferred to allow Delgado to accomplish calmly the shame and scandal which accompanied his victory in the 1988 Tour de France. In a haze during his most beautiful of years, Indurain waited patiently his turn, and his turn came in 1990, in the Luz-Ardiden uphill where Jose Miguel Echavarri understood that he didn't need to take care of the goats and the cabbages to choose between "Goya and Picasso," an expression he used to solve his dilemna.

"At the beginning of my career, I thought that my strong build would be terrible in the climb," Indurain said. "I saw myself more likely to be a classics racer. Then I met Professor Conconi, who convinced me to lose weight. Afterward, as a result of hard work and determination, and thanks to my rapid recuperative powers, I became a stage race specialist. But like anything in life, it did take time."

On the functional plane, the Spaniard presented a real phenomenon. In 1987, when Professor Conconi took him in for a check-up, he could not believe what the laboratory graphs showed. Miguel's lung capacity was superior to Merckx by nearly a liter, and his heart rate held to a slow rhythm of 28 beats per minute.

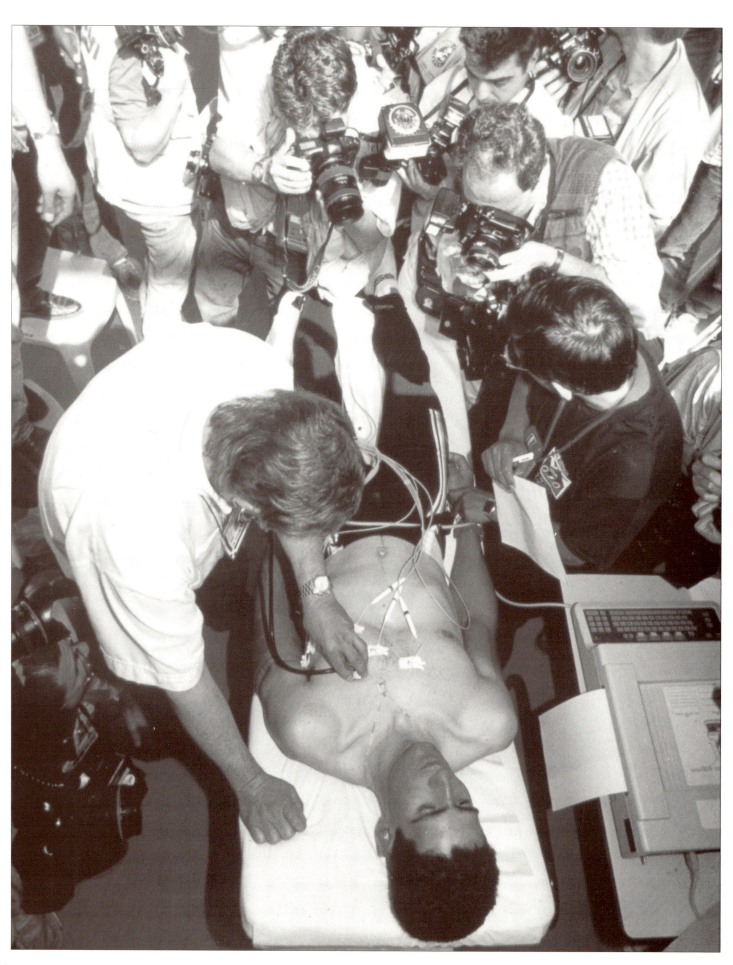

Four years of media superexposure have not erased the contours of a Robocop with a human face.

Five-time winner of the Tour, and holder of the time record (before Tony Rominger reclaimed it), Indurain defined himself as a typical champion, with his strong build, erect posture and long, tapered legs. He was different from the usual Iberian racers, who were usually small-boned with knotted legs. He represented the new kind of hero, capable of racing in the same manner as the French, Belgian, or Italian champions. Even though the political movement had already changed to Liberalism in Spain, with the Navaresse, its cycling climate entered full force into the modern era.

Reporters oftened compared Miguel to a robot, because his was not an expansive type of personality. He did not like to stand out from the crowd. Even with his futuristic helmet and space-age wheels, he did not like to project himself to the public as a futuristic vision of a cycling champion. He was much more traditional than that. However, under the reporters' eyes, nothing went unnoticed, noted his manager Echavarri. "Miguel Indurain worked hard to achieve what he has today. Each time he won the Tour and each time he reached tentative success against the time record, he provided us with a huge lesson in professionalism."

That farmer's son...what would he have become if it had not been for the sport of cycling which monopolized him? He was a contemplative leader in the sports media, where each big name was often asked their opinion. From him they received only silence, because he loved peace and quiet and the countryside. He relished the spectacle of the harvest under the clear skies of Navarre. This true champion did not understand why his opinion on anything would excite the passions of the public.

Again we are reminded of an interview he gave us, with frank and direct answers.

About Spanish reporters, he said, "I do not have a great rapport with them, because I am not a Spaniard in the traditional senese. I am not the exuberant type, I don't especially like bullfights. There is nothing I can do if I am a disappointment to them."

A word about his parents: "You know they are very religious and very simple people, they could care less about my celebrity."

And about you?

"Me, I never dreamed of becoming a star...never! If it wasn't that I am gifted in cycling, I would not have perservered in the sport."

Then why choose such a public job when you only like tranquility? His answer was sharp and direct:

"The tranquility is for later on!"

In 1991, when Indurain was preparing to win his first Tour de France, he already hated the crowds, the sham and the parades.

The Spaniard rarely spoke of his youth, his wife or his parents; not because of his modesty, but more likely his desire to keep his personal life private, his sanctuary untouched. We wondered what he did when he is not riding his bicycle. "He doesn't do anything, or almost anything," the Public Relations Manager affirmed. "What he likes above all else is to smell the scents of the farm."

His young wife Maria was as discreet as Miguel. She was employed at Pampelune University and refused to talk to reporters and Miguel's parents were no better. They lived between Irun and Pampelune at Villava, a small village, away from the cities which were prolific with trouble.

They farmed their 30 hectares of land which were divided into sections by rock walls. He had come from a profound and Catholic Spain, the Spain that had curled up with the traditional values that Francoism was unable to dissipate, and in one way this helped create the most recent big king of the Tour de France.

"Religion belongs in our history," Miguel said. "My parents never miss saying the rosary and myself, I go to church anytime I can. Faith is carrying me. Without it, I would certainly not have had the same success."

During the race, his mood was passive. "Sometimes he suffered like a martyr. For example, in 1991, on the road of Aix-les-Bains, nobody noticed his suffering, because he refused to show any emotion, as though he was wearing a mask," noted Pedro Delgado, a recent convert to journalism. The Navaresse managed his team without giving orders, he imposed order without asking his teammates. "He is so discreet, that when he leaves the dining table, we could not even hear him moving his chair," said Jean-Francois, who was Miguel's temporary teammate.

His strength consisted of just himself, while everything else invited him to capitalize on his name, his condition or his origin. He was an anachronistic star for whom glory made no difference. A multi-millionare, he could have escaped from the cold valleys of Navarre and settled down in a beautiful villa under the hot sun of the Costa Brava, but it was at Olaz where he chose to settle, two doors down from his parents at Villava. "I cannot see myself anywhere else than here," Miguel said.

Cycling champions are like that: they always remain loyal to their roots.

TOUR WINNERS

1903 Maurice Garin (France)	1954 Louison Bobet (France)
1904 Henri Cornet (France)	1955 Louison Bobet (France)
1905 Louis Trousselier (France)	1956 Roger Walkowiak (France)
1906 Rene Pottier (France)	1957 Jacques Anquetil (France)
1907 Lucien Petit-Breton (France)	1958 Charly Gaul (Luxembourg)
1908 Lucien Petit-Breton (France)	1959 Frederico Bahamontes (Spain)
1909 Francois Faber (Luxembourg)	1960 Gastone Nencini (Italy)
1910 Octave Lapize (France)	1961 Jacques Anquetil (France)
1911 Gustave Garrigou (France)	1962 Jacques Anquetil (France)
1912 Odile Defraye (Belgium)	1963 Jacques Anquetil (France)
1913 Philippe Thys (Belgium)	1964 Jacques Anquetil (France)
1914 Philippe Thys (Belgium)	1965 Felice Gimondi (Italy)
1915 - 1918 - *No race held*	1966 Lucien Aimar (France)
1919 Firmin Lambot (Belgium)	1967 Roger Pingeon (France)
1920 Philippe Thys (Belgium))	1968 Jan Janssen (Holland)
1921 Leon Scieur (Belgium)	1969 Eddy Merckx (Belgium)
1922 Firmin Lambot (France)	1970 Eddy Merckx (Belgium)
1923 Henri Pelissier (France)	1971 Eddy Merckx (Belgium)
1924 Ottavio Bottecchia (Italy)	1972 Eddy Merckx (Belgium)
1925 Ottavio Bottecchia (Italy)	1973 Luis Ocana (Spain)
1926 Lucien Buyze (Belgium)	1974 Eddy Merckx (Belgium)
1927 Nicolas Frantz (Luxembourg)	1975 Bernard Thevenet (France)
1928 Nicolas Frantz (Luxembourg)	1976 Lucien Van Impe (Belgium)
1929 Maurice DeWaele (Belgium)	1977 Bernard Thevenet (France)
1930 Andre LeDuco (France)	1978 Bernard Hinault (France)
1931 Antonin Magne (France)	1979 Bernard Hinault (France)
1932 Andre LeDuco (France)	1980 Joop Zotemelk (Holland)
1933 Georges Speicher (France)	1981 Bernard Hinault (France)
1934 Antonin Magne (France)	1982 Bernard Hinault (France)
1935 Romain Maes (Belgium)	1983 Laurent Fignon (France)
1936 Sylvere Maes (Belgium)	1984 Laurent Fignon (France)
1937 Roger Lapebie (France)	1985 Bernard Hinault (France)
1938 Gino Bartali (Italy)	1986 Greg LeMond (United States)
1939 Sylvere Maes (Belgium)	1987 Stephen Roche (Ireland)
1940 - 1946 - *No race held*	1988 Pedro Delgado (Spain)
1947 Jean Robic (France)	1989 Greg LeMond (United States)
1948 Gino Bartali (Italy)	1990 Greg LeMond (United States)
1949 Fausto Coppi (Italy)	1991 Miguel Indurain (Spain)
1950 Ferdinand Kubler (Switzerland)	1992 Miguel Indurain (Spain)
1951 Hugo Kublet (Switzerland)	1993 Miguel Indurain (Spain)
1952 Fausto Coppi (Italy)	1994 Miguel Indurain (Spain)
1953 Louison Bobet (France)	1995 Miguel Indurain (Spain)

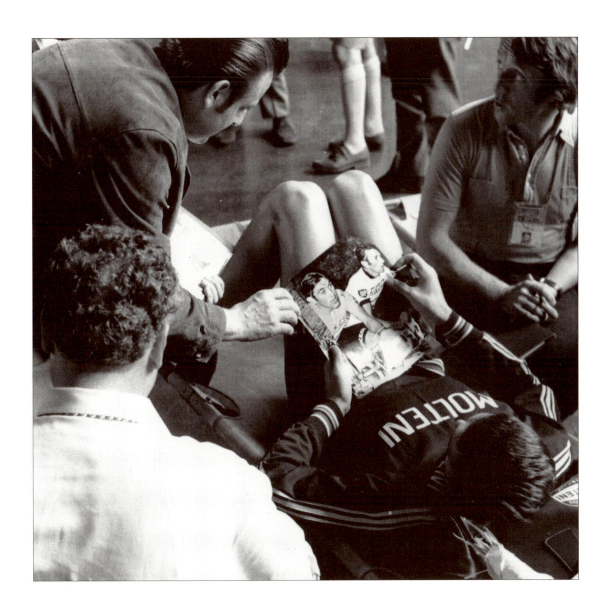

Acknowledgements

The author thanks all who participated in the book, particularly
Philippe Le Menn,
documentalist at *L'Equipe*, without whom this book would never have existed;

Jacques Augendre, Marc Jeuniau, Pierre Chany, Rino Negri and Mario Fossati for their contribution to the history of cycling;
La Gazetta dello Sport and *la Stampa*, which were very generous in giving access to their archives;

Ulysse Munoz, Fabrice Nicolle, Josyane Benassi, Jean-Michel Dubois, Philippe Pellerin and Xavier Watel,
workers in the photography laboratory at *L'Equipe*, for the excellent quality of their work;

the journal *L'Equipe*, which has permitted me to serve the Tour de France
and to rub elbows with a number of champions whose portraits are produced here.

Koblet abandons under the eyes of Jacques Goddet. A beautiful soldier takes his bow.